"I hope that as you read Heather's word[...] confidence and understanding of what it m[...] God's perfect will. I think you will find that no matter your situation, He has you right where you belong."

from the foreword by **Candace Cameron Bure**, actress, producer, and *New York Times* bestselling author

"With tenacious relentlessness, Heather shepherds moms of all shapes and sizes to the wholehearted understanding that we are exactly the mothers God wants for our children. No one gets left behind, not on Heather's watch. She reminds us that we don't have to fit into a certain box to be a good mom; we just have to trust where God has placed our boundary lines and joyfully operate within them."

Erin Moon, author and resident Bible scholar for *The Bible Binge* podcast

"The greatest gift I've ever received was the permission to be fully myself. And in *Right Where You Belong*, Heather not only gives the reader that permission but also invites us into a vulnerable step-by-step journey to discovering where our fully embraced selves can dwell and activate our God-given purpose. This book is freeing, honest, and incredibly helpful."

Toni Collier, speaker, author of *Brave Enough to Be Broken*, and podcast host

"As Jesus followers, we are called to 'find REST for our weary souls' and 'RUN the race marked out for us.' But few of us know how to both rest and run well—myself included! Which is why I'm honored to recommend *Right Where You Belong*. Heather's writing is woven with great insight and biblical instruction to help us live a more fulfilling and Spirit-empowered life in whatever season or space we are currently in. If you know the tension of feeling like you're either doing too much or not doing enough for the kingdom, this is the book you've been waiting for!"

Jeannie Cunnion, author of *Don't Miss Out*

"God has called me lower, higher, wider, and deeper than I could have ever imagined. And in each new space and place, I've been humbled and lifted up. In all of that stretching, God has convinced me that He has a plan for my life that He is working. Join my friend Heather as she helps you understand, inhabit, and grow in your God-given spaces and places."

Jonathan Pitts, cofounder of For Girls Like You ministries

RIGHT
WHERE
YOU
BELONG

RIGHT
WHERE
YOU
BELONG

How to Identify and Fully Occupy
Your God-Given Space

Heather MacFadyen

Revell
a division of Baker Publishing Group
Grand Rapids, Michigan

Published by Revell
a division of Baker Publishing Group
Grand Rapids, MI
www.revellbooks.com

Printed in the United States of America

Library of Congress Cataloging-in-Publication Data
Names: MacFadyen, Heather C., 1977– author.
Title: Right where you belong : how to identify and fully occupy your God-given space / Heather MacFadyen.
Description: Grand Rapids, MI : Revell, a division of Baker Publishing Group, [2023] | Includes bibliographical references.
Identifiers: LCCN 2022031027 | ISBN 9780800739317 (paperback) | ISBN 9780800742898 (casebound) | ISBN 9781493439805 (ebook)
Subjects: LCSH: Vocation—Christianity. | Identity (Psychology)—Religious aspects—Christianity.
Classification: LCC BV4740 .M22 2023 | DDC 230.0023—dc23/eng/20221011
LC record available at https://lccn.loc.gov/2022031027

23 24 25 26 27 28 29   7 6 5 4 3 2 1

FOR MY MOM,

who continually embraces the spaces God gives her,
whether they feel like a palace or a prison.
Your lived-out faith and consistent obedience prove to me
that a life poured out for Christ is worth the cost.
"To live is Christ, and to die is gain" (Phil. 1:21 ESV).
Thank you for not only giving me life
(even if it was a surprise)
but giving me a life of belonging.

Contents

Contents

Foreword

Like any working mom, I've spent my fair share of time wondering if I was getting it right. Not just the mom part—that pressure is enough all on its own—but the other questions seemed endless. Am I making the right business decision leaving a successful career to stay home with my kids? Am I missing out on something because I got married at twenty and didn't choose the same path as other women my age? Will I act again, and if I do, will they embrace me? Will my husband still want to be with me if we can't survive the teenage parenting years? Will I still want to be with him?

What Heather has to say about these kinds of questions and the challenges we face is important. She gives us endless encouragement from her own experience, along with a plan that works and isn't one-size-fits-all.

Like yours, my story is still being written. My kids are young adults now, and I'm thriving as the CEO of several businesses as I continue to produce, direct, and act in television and films. But one of the only reasons I can say I am thriving is because of the people who showed me how to keep my priorities straight. My parents set a great example for me and my siblings. No one is perfect, but as they worked through their own challenges, I saw examples of how to find purpose and a strong rhythm of balance in the ever-changing seasons of life. My husband, Val, and I are trying our best to pass on the same lessons to our children.

When I was young, my mom didn't have an in-office career the way my dad did as a public schoolteacher. When I began acting at the age of five, my mom was figuring out how to balance running four kids to and from school, auditions, and work on set, all the while maintaining that her first priority was to keep my siblings and me grounded. The entertainment industry can be chaotic, and she knew early on that she didn't want her kids to be arrogant, spoiled child stars. So she and my dad worked hard to protect us.

If we went to an audition and didn't get the part, she taught us to have confidence regardless of the outcome because we had done our best. I know this steady hand came because God gave her confidence and guidance even though she was still figuring it out and didn't have all the answers. She showed up fully for that season of being a mom of four children with different schedules, different schools, and the attention of Hollywood.

Once my brother and I got busier with our respective television shows, it was clear we were going to need professional management—and my mom stepped right up. She looked at the opportunity in front of her and considered what was best for our family and for us kids individually, along with the experience she'd gained over the years. Then she went for it! She became our manager and eventually went on to open the Barbara Cameron Talent Agency. It would have been easy just to hire a professional who knew the industry, but I will always be grateful that my mom kept her first priority: to look after the well-being of us four kids and protect us as she navigated our careers and home life. I know that one of the reasons I am the successful businesswoman, mother, and wife I am today is because of her guidance and leadership.

I imagine that once she stepped into a full-time job, life got a bit crazier. But I didn't notice any chaos. I think that's because my dad and mom both had their priorities clear—having a healthy family came first. Spending quality time together, having fun, doing the important but mundane chores, and supporting each other were number one for them. This is a legacy that has carried over to the way Val and I have lived. Of course things get hectic, but quality time with family will always be more important than a career.

You might be reading this book as someone who doesn't have their own children, but I know this: You almost surely have young people in your life who look up to you. And part of discovering how to bring your best self to your life and your work will involve shaping the way those young individuals become healthy adults— who in turn will pass on what they have learned from you.

God gave each of us unique gifts and paths to travel in life. Unique not because someone else can't do the same job we do but because our exact mixes of experiences and interests are so different. I was born in Los Angeles, California, and started acting at age five. My husband was born in Moscow, Russia, while it was the Soviet Union, where he started playing hockey at age three. And somehow we ended up together! We both learned to work hard when we were little, and that has continued to shape us into who we are today. But we both could have gone in completely different directions because the choices we have in life are endless.

I firmly believe that you can do everything you want; you just can't do everything well at the same time. You will always have to choose something and let go of another. But don't worry, it will be there for you to pick up again in another season of life! I hope as you read Heather's words, you'll gain a deeper confidence and understanding of what it means for you to live in God's perfect will. I think you will find that no matter your situation, He has you right where you belong.

Candace Cameron Bure

Introduction

My Space

"I'm so stupid."

At my request Bruce had shown me a spreadsheet of our income and expenses. My immediate reaction was shame. I thought podcasting and writing would not only offer encouragement to others but also help provide significant income to our family.

Why had I drifted away from my speech-language pathology (SLP) career? If I'd stuck with it, I could have been making a decent income. Our family could have traveled, done some home renovations, bought new clothes, etc. Yet I foolishly started writing online, then recording podcast episodes, and now writing books. None of which appeared to offer my family the first-world-level financial position I imagined would bring elusive contentment.

I climbed back into bed at 8:20 a.m. and bawled.

How could I work my way out of the commitments I'd made? Podcast ads were booked for the next nine months. My second manuscript was due in just three weeks, and it would be another year before this book launched.

A layer of anger came when I thought about the sacrifices of my time and energy. They felt like a waste. Plenty of other people create podcasts and books to encourage moms. If the things I created weren't around, someone else's work would fill the space. Basically, I could have pursued my career as an SLP and the world would have kept spinning.

My husband, Bruce, sat next to me on the bed, with its tear-stained sheets, and listened to me vent all my frustrations.

"I'm so sorry. I'm so sorry. I don't know why I thought ministry was a good idea," I said. My pity party spilled into questioning all my roles: *I'm a terrible friend because of the time I put into this ministry. I'm a subpar mom. I'm not even the kind of wife I'd like to be.* And then I realized my meltdown was going to make us late for church. There was no way I was going to let that happen and add guilt to this shame storm.

I popped out of the bed and grabbed a frozen facial roller to attempt to tame the puffiness under my eyes. After I quickly straightened my hair and applied loads of concealer, we made our way to church. On the way, I said a little prayer: *Lord, I know You don't have to, but if You could send me a few reminders that my last ten years haven't been in vain, I would greatly appreciate it.*

Although the sermon wasn't given by our primary pastor, the words offered what I needed. He said, verbatim, "You can trust God with the results. If you are working as hard as you can for God and wonder if anyone sees you, if it matters at all, God sees you. God honors those who honor Him. Even if you don't see the outcome in this lifetime, He sees your heart, your sacrifices, and your dedication to Him." Then the pastor encouraged us to internalize the priorities of God.

I realized that God's priorities do not include the comfort and convenience of extra cash. He desires dependence on Him. He cares about me offering my gifts and abilities in service to His work. Maybe in the future that will include a career in speech-language pathology again. But I know without a doubt that I have faithfully followed each step God has placed before me to get where I am today. I have honored Him. I have identified and fully occupied my God-given space.

After processing my meltdown, I can confidently say I'm right where I belong.

This book is the message I've been given to steward. On these pages you'll find an invitation to live "rightsized," to be encouraged if your life story isn't turning out the way you thought it would or isn't following the mold of what you've been told is "right and good." I want to help you toss aside insecurities and step up to fill whatever space you have been assigned, whether your daily activities don't feel important enough or a next step seems bigger than your ability.

I've shared this message with a group of eighth-grade girls deciding how they want to enter their next space of high school. I've discussed it with my pastor to encourage him to step into his next big assignment. I've encouraged groups of moms with young kids to trust that their realities are not the end of their stories. I've talked about it with friends while crying over coffee about their broken marriages and their pain not being wasted.

I hope that in these pages, by sharing my experiences and the things God has taught me, I can help sharpen your discernment to give you confidence in God's assignments for your life. And I hope you experience contentment in occupying the space He's giving you. That you'll believe it is right and good because God is with you and has never left you. You'll feel true belonging outside of any structure or human-made entity or fallible relationship. It's my hope that in time you'll move past simple belonging and fill that space with the authority God has given you as His daughter, coheir with Christ, and member of the royal priesthood. That you'll create spiritual waves in an unseen dimension with outcomes you may never see with your physical eyes.

I believe God wants us to know these truths. He wants us to feel peace. He wants us to drop the need to hustle. He wants us to increase our faith, trusting that He's in control, and to know we'll never miss out if we are in the middle of His sovereign will for us.

Never Missing Out

> Hoping does not mean doing nothing. It is not fatalistic resignation. It means going about our assigned task, confident that God will provide the meaning and the conclusions.
>
> Eugene Peterson

My cat keeps trying to escape our house.

I don't think she's paid attention to the Nextdoor posts about coyote sightings. Or even our eyewitness accounts, like the other night when loud crying woke my husband and me from a deep sleep around 2:00 a.m. When Bruce went to investigate, he saw two coyotes fighting/mating in our front yard. Y'all, we live one block from a major highway in Dallas, Texas. This makes no sense. Nonetheless, our petite kitty, Eliza Hamilton, thinks she's fit for the dangers beyond our back door. Here's what I keep wondering: Is it really that bad in our home? Don't we provide everything she needs for life, liberty, and the pursuit of happiness in her little cat life: food, water, and toilet?

And yet there's a part of me that can relate to her kitty angst. From third through eighth grade, my homeschooled heart longed for more. Those years of yearning hardwired me to think, *Life is better somewhere else.* My homeschool soundtrack could have included "Part of Your World" from *The Little Mermaid*. I spent hours memorizing the lyrics and performing it on my bed in front of the audience of my mirror. You may be less familiar with the song, so let me share a few of the lyrics: "I want to be where the people are. . . . Wish I could be part of that world." Just swap the ocean with my bedroom and you can see how Ariel and I were basically soul sisters.

This thought pattern started before social media existed. But one scroll on Instagram can bring a litany of similar lies to the surface and cause my discontent to rise. Seeing perfectly curated highlight-reel pictures, I repeatedly hear the phrase, *I'm missing out.*

The woman I admire preaching from a stage. *I'm missing out.*

A group of my friends sharing lunch. *I'm missing out.*

Her daughter qualifying for the national team. *I'm missing out.*

The family serving on a mission trip together. *I'm missing out.*

Is being a mom enough? Are my efforts enough? Am I missing a special skill that would make this experience as easy as it looks like it is for her? Should I start an online "fill-in-the-blank" like she did? Do I struggle with my kids because I didn't read enough, play enough, serve them enough organic food? Did I make a mistake pulling back from my career to stay home full-time? Will I ever be "successful," or did I miss that opportunity? Most importantly, have I missed my calling?

Exhausting.

If you have felt the crushing weight of believing you're not enough or too much, you are not alone. Authors Jess Connolly and Hayley Morgan write,

Women are living defensively, all bound up by their own fears and self-imposed limitations. When we feel like we're not enough, we try to puff ourselves up and get big. It's easy in a world that says "Do big things!" to feel like you don't measure up. On the other hand, when we feel like we're way too much, it can be tempting to get low, even if it's with a self-serving false humility. These are two sides of the same coin, and I feel both too much and never enough all the time.[1]

To add to the pressure, we're often handed contradictory advice. Some self-help gurus chant "work harder" and "hustle to make it happen"! Other influencers suggest the answer is to pull back, get smaller, and rest. There has to be a third option. A way for everyone to combat FOMO (the fear of missing out).

An Age-Old Question

A layer of freedom came for me when God introduced a new way of thinking. He desired better for me, and He desires better for you as well. I was working through a twenty-one-day soul detox. One of the exercises in the program was to chronicle thoughts you've had for the past twenty-four hours. Most likely you can think of three or four dominant thoughts. While journaling mine, through prayer and the power of the Holy Spirit, the negative thought pattern of FOMO stood out. The next exercise was to help replace the fear with truth and ask God, "What do You want me to think instead?"

That's when He brought to mind this truth: *If you are in the middle of My will, then you are never missing out.* What a relief! So, the next step in the detox protocol was to apply that truth in my everyday moments. Each time an event, Instagram post, or conversation started to bring up the thought, *I'm missing out*, I would stop and take that thought captive. Then I would replace it with the truth God had given me: *If you are in the middle of My will, then*

21

you are never missing out. With my career. With my marriage. With my kids. With my friendships. I'm never going to miss out.

One problem: How do I know what God's will is? Not only is it a big question, but I'm also not the first to ask it. In fact, knowing God's will has been a conundrum discussed for centuries. In college I remember working through the popular Bible study *Experiencing God: Knowing and Doing the Will of God* by Henry and Richard Blackaby and Claude V. King. The study focuses on the life of Moses and the idea that to know God is to experience Him. They point out that we often ask, "What is God's will for my life?" but a better question is, "What's God's will and how can I join Him?" We can do that by looking for where God is at work, listening for His invitation, and choosing to join Him.[2] On the cover of the study is a picture of Moses at the burning bush, an example of how God revealed Himself and His work and extended an invitation to Moses.

In their book *Seven Realities for Experiencing God*, the Blackabys say,

> God was already at work around Moses' life when He encountered Moses at the burning bush. God had a purpose He was steadily working out in Moses' world. Even though Moses was an exile in the desert, he was right on God's schedule, in the fullness of God's timing, in the middle of God's will for that moment.
>
> Years earlier God told Abraham that his descendants would be in bondage but that He would deliver them and give them the promised land. God was watching and waiting for the right time to carry out His purpose for Israel.
>
> At the time God was about to deliver the children of Israel, the overriding concern was His will for Israel, not His will for Moses. God was at work with Israel, and He was preparing to bring Moses into the mainstream of His activity to redeem His people.[3]

There was a bigger plan than God's will for Moses. He had a rescue plan for you and me, and that started with His chosen people, the Israelites. Moses was a player in that big plan. It was God's presence that made the encounter holy, or set apart. The bush wasn't holy until God dwelt there. One piece of figuring out God's will is to focus on His presence and bigger plan. Instead of asking, *Am I missing out?* more satisfaction comes by asking, *Am I in the middle of where God is working, and how is He inviting me to join Him?*

When I was five years old, I stood with my mom watching a local parade. The excitement of the marching band and candy being flung out to the crowds from the floats made my little heart so happy. But it was when I saw my dad sitting in one of the passing convertibles that I began to jump up and down. He gestured for me to come and join him. My mom led me to the car, and I climbed inside to smile and wave at the crowd for the rest of the parade route. An unforgettable experience to share with my dad.

I now know that, at the time, my dad was campaigning for the U.S. Congress. Obviously, his campaign success didn't depend on how well I waved from the convertible. He didn't need my help to capture more votes (although I bet I was pretty adorable). He invited me because of his love for me and his desire to deepen our connection. The same is true of God. He doesn't need us to accomplish His redemptive plan, but He invites us to join Him.

Assigned, Not Smooshed

"We can't be smooshed by God."

My youngest son is a verbal processor. Sadly, most of the time I'm not listening. Particularly on the days when he would get out of school three hours before his brothers and it was just him and me. Often the conversation consisted of his monologues and my *uh-huh*s.

The other day I happened to tune in when he said, "I was talking to my friends about how God is everywhere, but we can't get smooshed by God. And I don't think they understood what I meant."

Impressed by my mini-theologian, I responded with, "Man, that's an amazing observation. And I totally understand what you're saying. God *is* everywhere. And in order for us to live in His presence, God makes space for us."

He excitedly agreed. "And that's why we don't get smooshed."

We don't get smooshed. But I've had several conversations with women who feel crushed by the weight of discovering their purpose. They stress over the question, *What's my calling?* Figuring out who they are and why they exist consumes their thoughts, time, and energy. Maybe you feel the same way. Or perhaps you look around at your reality and wonder, *Did I miss my calling?*

During a podcast interview, my friend Kat Armstrong helped release a bit of the purpose-seeking burden by clarifying the term *calling*. She said that as followers of Christ we have been given the same calling He gave His apostles to "go and make disciples" (Matt. 28:19 NIV). Kat went on to say, "The various places *where* we fulfill that calling are our assignments."[4]

Those assignments will shift and change over the course of a lifetime. I love *The Message*'s version of 1 Corinthians 7:17: "And don't be wishing you were someplace else or with someone else. Where you are right now is God's place for you. Live and obey and love and believe right there." The ESV says, "Let each person lead the life that the Lord has assigned to him." What a gift that each person's assignment will look different from someone else's.

When I think about God making space for us, and assignments over callings, the Garden of Eden comes to mind. Adam and Eve experienced perfect communion with God in the first assignment of the Garden. Unfortunately, like me, they believed the lie of "missing out" and ate fruit from the tree of the knowledge of good and evil. That act of choosing their own way tainted the rest of humanity's relationship with God. His love for the world did not change—but the arrangement was altered. Adam and Eve could no longer dwell in the space God had assigned them. If they would have stayed, eating from the tree of life after eating from the tree of the knowledge of good and evil would have kept them eternally separated from God.

So begins the story of God's plan to redeem that relationship. To bring us back into communion with Him. It is a journey that requires setting apart a group of people from all the other people. To deliver our Rescuer, the Messiah, into this world, God chooses and assigns the Israelites, a group of people who find their origin in a man named Abram.

God calls Abram from his hometown and directs him to an assigned land. He promises that Abram will be the father of many (more than the stars in the sky) and that the world will be blessed through him. In connection with this covenant, God renames Abram ("exalted father") Abraham ("father of a multitude").

Abraham believes God and moves to the place God has directed him. Of course, being human, Abraham has a lot of missteps along the way because he fears he's missing out. Trying to avoid being killed, he tells the Egyptians his wife, Sarah, is his sister. Later he has a son with his wife's maidservant because he's worried he will miss out on having descendants. Now, there are times Abraham does take risks and trust that God will fulfill His promise, even if the circumstances are questionable (e.g., when Abraham is willing to sacrifice his only son, Isaac).

Fast-forward in the story, and Abraham's son Isaac has twin sons, Jacob and Esau. Out of fear of missing out on a blessing and inheritance, Jacob tricks his brother, Esau, and lies to their father, Isaac. The story continues with Jacob's sons being intimidated by their brother Joseph and his dreams. Joseph's dreams predict all the brothers will bow down to him in his assigned space of honor and authority.

Taking matters in their own hands, they sell Joseph to be a slave. Even though their decision is motivated by fear and anger, God works through that situation. Joseph's assignment in Egypt and his place in prison leads him to interpret Pharaoh's dreams. Pharaoh places Joseph in charge of managing the seven years of plenty to allow for the seven years of famine that are coming to the land. Joseph's family—his eleven brothers, the sons of Jacob/Israel—moves to Egypt to survive.

All the fears of missing out could not stop God's plan for the protection of these chosen people and the ultimate rescue of the whole world.

We find our way back to Moses. From a burning bush, God invites and assigns Moses to join Him in leading the Israelites out of Egypt and their position of slavery. God's presence goes with Moses and the Israelites as they travel toward the land God promised them. "The LORD went in front of them in a pillar of cloud by day, to lead them along the way, and in a pillar of fire by night, to give them light, so that they might travel by day and by night" (Exod. 13:21).

When we see "LORD" with all capital letters in the Old Testament, it is the Hebrew name for God, Yahweh, which means "I AM." It's a present-tense verb that represents God's presence with Moses as he fulfills his assigned leadership role and God's presence with the Israelites as they occupy the space He has assigned them.

Further on, in Exodus 35–40, we read about the building of the tabernacle. How the Spirit of God fills two men, Bezalel and Oholiab, to use their gifts, skills, and intelligence to design and craft the tabernacle and the ark of the covenant, the place where God's presence will rest. "The glory of the LORD filled the tabernacle. . . . Whenever the cloud was taken up from the tabernacle, the Israelites would set out on each stage of their journey" (Exod. 40:34, 36).

After settling into the promised land, the Israelites begged for a king. We'll discuss their first king later. God assigned David to be the second king of Israel.

David is the youngest of his seven brothers and from the smallest tribe. Although he is a man after God's own heart, his missteps lead to his not being assigned the task of building a permanent structure for God's presence to dwell. It is his son King Solomon who obeys the instructions to build a house for the Lord, the temple in Jerusalem. But God is clear with Solomon. Building the temple does not secure God's presence. "If you turn aside from following me, you or your children, and do not keep my commandments and my statutes that I have set before you but go and serve other gods and worship them, then I will cut Israel off from the land that I have given them. . . . This house will become a heap of ruins" (1 Kings 9:6–8).

Unfortunately, Israel didn't keep God's commandments, and they did choose to worship other gods. And the temple was destroyed. But their lack of faithfulness did not cause God's plan to fail. "For God so loved the world that he gave his only Son, so that everyone who believes in him may not perish but may have eternal life. Indeed, God did not send the Son into the world to condemn the world but in order that the world might be saved through him" (John 3:16–17). God assigned Christ to fill a baby's body. Christ, fully God and fully human, walked the earth, bringing God's presence to dwell among His people.

While God's presence in a cloud led the Israelites along *their* way, Christ invites us to experience God more fully as we go along our way. He says, "I *am the way* and the truth and the life. No one comes to the Father except through me" (John 14:6, emphasis added). Christ took His assigned space on the cross, understanding it was required to take on the consequence of sin for us. To bring us back into relationship with God required a perfect sacrifice. He was the only one without sin who could be that sacrifice for us. Being God, Jesus had the power to conquer death. The best news is that belief in His resurrection brings us the greatest gift to keep us in the middle of God's will—His presence *in* us.

Over and over in the Old Testament, God instructed the Israelites to keep His laws so that His presence would remain with them. Then in the New Testament, Jesus starts not with the law but with love. "If you love me, you will keep my commandments.

And I will ask the Father, and he will give you another Helper, to be with you forever" (John 14:15–16 ESV). That Helper, the Holy Spirit, resides in us and guides us to fulfill our callings in our various assignments. "Peace be with you. As the Father has sent me, so I send you. . . . Receive the Holy Spirit" (20:21–22).

As my son pointed out, we are not smooshed by God. He loves us so much that He is willing to make room for us. He invites us into His greater plan and calls us to be on mission with Him. Beyond that, God desires to walk in relationship with us. So He sent His Son to earth to redeem us. And we are the ones who get to make room for Jesus in our souls.

I call it a God sandwich. God all around us and God in us. Like Jesus says, "I am in my Father, and you in me, and I in you" (14:20). Because of our faith in Jesus, we get to enjoy God's presence around us and in us *forever*. So, as believers we never miss out. We are fully in the middle of His presence, empowered to accomplish our various assignments.

He'll Meet You There

Remember how my cat longed to frolic outside with the coyotes, and I wanted to be set free from my homeschool prison? I can relate to my cat's love for the outdoors. During those homeschool years, my favorite place to meet with God was in the acres of woods behind my childhood home. I'd spend hours climbing trees, listening to the wind blow through the branches and rustle the leaves. Or sitting on the creek bed watching water rush over rocks and sometimes letting it cool my bare feet. Being surrounded by nature has always centered my heart.

If you've ever been to the mountains and felt their comparative enormity or stood on the edge of the ocean and looked out over the never-ending waves, then maybe you have experienced a similar awe that nature can bring. When I stand under the vast nighttime sky filled with stars, God's handiwork gives me the security that He knows what He is doing. He is in control, and I can trust Him.

I recently heard the story of Vaneetha Risner, who lives with disabilities from childhood polio. She had over two dozen surgeries as a child and has experienced many heartaches in her lifetime. Vaneetha had read countless devotionals on how God speaks through nature, and she longed to experience Him in that way. But her inability to navigate the terrain independently prevented her from that experience, which made her feel like she was missing out.

Until one day when a friend helped her to a bench facing a beautiful waterfall in the woods. Unfortunately, she discovered that the reality fell short of her expectation. After trying for over an hour to have a meaningful faith experience, Vaneetha was helped back inside, frustrated that everything in her life had to be hard. Wondering why God showed up for other people but not for her, she sat down at a desk and opened her Bible to the same passage she'd been reading outside. This time the words jumped off the page. She felt encouraged and embraced by God's presence. Vaneetha notes, "I wasn't missing out. I didn't need to go anywhere special to experience God. He wanted to meet me where I was. In a way that was readily accessible to me. I didn't need to feel jealous that other people climbed mountains and sat by beautiful streams to commune with God. God meets me in different ways."[5]

This is the beauty of focusing on experiencing God. Your path will be different from mine. Your way of experiencing Him will be different from mine. There's freedom in knowing God's desire is a relationship with you. The only way you miss out is if you don't accept His invitation to join Him.

Paul asks, "Is there any encouragement from belonging to Christ?" (Phil. 2:1 NLT). I would respond with absolutely yes! There is no other person or place that is better to belong to than Christ.

While I can't go back and encourage my yearning middle-school self, it's comforting to me now to know that she wasn't missing a thing. The hours spent connecting with God in nature weren't wasted. Her assignments were just getting started. There was so much more God had in store than she could ever have imagined.

DISCUSSION QUESTIONS

1. When have you felt the fear of missing out?
2. How would it have helped you in that season to refocus your thoughts to being in the middle of God's will?
3. What is your preferred way of connecting with God's presence? Why do you think that is?
4. How does it impact your heart and mind to pay attention to God's assignments instead of worrying about your calling?
5. In considering your place of belonging, how does the image of being in the middle of a "God sandwich" encourage you?

Humbled Success

It is a great paradox in Christianity that it makes humility the avenue to glory.

M. G. Easton

I would rather learn to quilt than write a book.

The irony is that by choosing quilting over writing, I'm not living out the whole point of this book's message. *So why do I keep hitting these keys?*

Let me explain by addressing the quilting first. Perhaps you're wondering if I wrote this book in the 1800s. Nope. I'm just so hip and cool, I want to learn how to quilt for fun. (This is when I wish formal publications allowed emojis. I would definitely be winking at you right now.)

Truth is, at this moment I'm sitting in a large room full of folding tables arranged in rows. Twenty of my friends from church and I have descended upon a little bed-and-breakfast in Rainbow, Texas, for our annual craft retreat.

Every gal arrived at the retreat with her projects in hand, ready to settle into her assigned crafting area. Each six-foot-long table is equipped with a desk lamp, power strip, hanging trash can, and cup holder. Three days to eat food we didn't cook, wear comfy clothes, watch chick flicks, sleep in late, and create.

From my vantage point, I can see the whole room. Women who are focused on projects. Two friends chatting in the corner. Another sneaking over to the snack table for one more handful of chocolate-covered almonds. (I think about doing the same.)

For some of you, a craft retreat sounds like a dreamy scenario. Others of you are cringing at the thought, wondering what you would work on at your table. Maybe you feel a bit of shame for not having a skill set or hobby that you could spend days doing. Or you're cursing your mom for never teaching you how to sew. ("Come on, Mom!")

What amazes me every year is the variety of choices my friends bring to the table. From scrapbooking to crocheting, website design, writing, or weaving, each one pursues her interest. And there's chatter throughout the day, oohing and aahing over each other's work. Appreciating the colorful blend of fabrics in a quilt, the intricate design of a crocheted blanket, the adorable array of family pictures.

You'll also hear, "I'm so impressed, but I could never do that." I might even look across the room and wonder why I'd rather make something with my hands than strategically plan out the next year's calendar (yes, this is actually an activity some women do). Or why someone else would rather organize a computer's hard drive than weave a lampshade (this is also a thing). Some of us will leave this weekend considering if we should learn a new skill. In that momentary musing, we'll slide down the slippery slope of "should," ignoring the oft-repeated warning, "Comparison is the thief of self-contentment."[1]

Truly, the most contented crafters at the retreat keep their eyes fixed on a few things. They know their interests and giftings and bring projects to maximize their talents. They don't get distracted by comparison. Instead, they take time to encourage a friend or enjoy a walk around the property. They fill their assigned crafting space.

There's a similar need in our assigned God-given spaces. Not only to stay within our spaces but to occupy them fully, acknowledging the gifts, resources, time, and experiences we each bring to the table. In my experience, many women falter in owning their place, including myself.

Stranded Nobody

A few years ago, one of my dear friends, Jenn, arrived at the craft retreat a bit weary from homeschooling her four children. Happy to have a weekend away from her normal responsibilities, she chose not to bring anything to work on at her table. After a day of sitting and watching the rest of us busy ourselves with projects, she decided to go on an adventure. A canoeing adventure, no less.

She headed to a local canoe-rental company and made her way down the river. All was going well—until it wasn't.

The river they sent her down was managed. Meaning the dam was opened, filling the riverbed with water, then closed off. The farther she went on her journey, the lower the water level dropped, like a draining bathtub, until she sat in a canoe in a waterless riverbed and cried to her husband on the phone. While she in no way found this situation humorous, her husband giggled when he heard the name of the business: the Low Water canoe company in Nemo, Texas.

Yep. Sitting in a waterless riverbed in a canoe rented from the Low Water canoe company. An all-time low. (Pun most definitely intended.) You see, Jenn had already been on quite a journey. Years prior, she'd felt God's leading to complete medical school prerequisites. But during a visit to a medical school, she made the decision to stop pursuing that assignment. Something didn't sit right with her, so instead of becoming a doctor, she returned home to care for her four kiddos full-time.

Jenn arrived at the craft retreat questioning her purpose and bringing "nothing to the table." She then attempted to seek out significance via the solo canoe trip, only to hit a literal low in the town of Nemo.

Did you know *nemo* is Latin for "nobody"? A title that reinforced the lie she was believing: "I'm a nobody. If I'm not pursuing God's will to become a doctor, how could God use me?" She was feeling stuck and stranded. And not just physically.

Can you relate? Have you felt purposeless, wondering if your daily activities have meaning? Maybe you feel like you have over-extended yourself and you are one mistake away from a break-down? In trying to make a name for yourself, you've hustled and strived and found your current reality as empty as the riverbed Jenn found herself in. So many of us ask the question, "Do I matter?" then spend our lives trying to prove that we do. Often, we answer that question through relentlessly performing, garnering people's acceptance, or gathering possessions.

Like when I sat in our first apartment, overlooking downtown Wheaton, Illinois. I wondered if I'd made a mistake graduating a semester early and moving our wedding up from June to March. Wasn't marriage considered to be an exciting life milestone? Yet here I was alone in a new town while my friends made incredible last-semester-of-college memories. And my husband, whom I couldn't wait to be with, traveled for work three weeks out of the month. My biology/premedicine degree went unused as I lived the unemployed life instead of attending medical school. Without a place to perform or relationships to feed off, what value did I have?

I remember one of the rare nights Bruce was in town. He sat out in the living room with his former roommates brainstorming a refrigerator that would track grocery use. This Jetson-esque fridge would not only track but reorder items as needed (this was 1999, BTW). In hindsight I can appreciate his ingenuity and entrepreneurial spirit. But at the time, instead of joining in their lively conversation, I sat in our bedroom and cried. How was this my life? I missed my friends. I missed having a planned-out trajectory and purpose. Like Jenn, I felt like a stranded nobody. Was this what being humbled felt like? If so, it was for the birds.

One of the Hebrew words for "humble" is *ani*.[2] It means "circumstantial humility." It's used in the Old Testament when someone suffers or has been afflicted. They find themselves in a lowly position physically, materially, socially. While I knew that many people suffered much lower positions than I was experiencing, I think I had found myself in a circumstance lower than my expectation. That was humbling.

Ani in circumstance often leads to another Hebrew word, *anav*, which relates to humble character.[3] Being needy (*ani*) causes a gal to depend on God to meet her needs. In doing so, she becomes humble (*anav*) in the dependence process. In her weak, underdog position, she becomes aware of her need and inability to change people, circumstances, or outcomes. Thankfully, we have Someone who fights on our behalf. Over and over in the Old Testament, God shares how He cares for the humble. He guides the *anav* (Ps. 25:9). He crowns the *anav* with salvation (149:4). He encourages the *anav* (34:2). The reward? The *anav* inherits the land (37:11).

That last verse about inheriting the land reminds me of a tweet that sparked the whole concept for this book. Yes, a tweet. It was posted by Bobby Gruenewald, the creator of the YouVersion Bible App, but he was quoting a YouVersion devotional written by Pastor Dave Adamson: "The Hebrew word 'avanah' is translated as 'humility.' But an expanded translation would be to occupy our God-given space. Humility is not just avoiding overstepping our boundaries, but it's also being sure we step into them."[4]

Let me repeat it, because I've been thinking about this concept for years and I want to make sure you and I are on the same page. Humility isn't just about hard circumstances or developing a character trait. According to Adamson, an expanded translation of *humility* is "to occupy our God-given space." *To occupy our God-given space.*

Turn the Crank

Now, I didn't want to take a tweet or devotional entry as fact, so you know your girl hit up Google to do some more research. First of all, when I couldn't find anything on *avanah*, I discovered Dave may have accidentally misspelled the Hebrew word *anavah*—a little letter swap of *n* and *v*. If you glance back up a few paragraphs, perhaps you've already noticed how *anavah* is an expanded form of *anav*, the Hebrew word for those of "humble character." What I appreciate about the expanded form is how it emphasizes that humility isn't about getting smaller but about trusting God with where you are, even if it feels like a step backward.

In my situation, in a new town with an unused degree, no community, and a traveling husband, the imagined space I had drawn up for myself did not match my reality. So I humbly looked at the space God gave me, and I chose to fill it. The first step involved taking a job as a teacher's assistant in West Chicago. While I was grateful to a friend for sending me the opportunity, it felt like a step backward. I had been on a path to get my medical degree. Instead, I was offered a job that required only a high school diploma.

You know what was even more humbling? Despite years of babysitting and working with kids, I didn't know what I was doing as a teacher's assistant. I had to ask a lot of questions and be open to a lot of training. *But* by occupying that God-given space, I met a student named Andrew. The lessons he taught me are forever imprinted on my heart.

Part of my job was to help Andrew navigate his school day, particularly when he would get upset and perseverate on a situation. One tactic involved imagining a mechanical crank in his head. (He loved engineering.) When a situation made him upset, he and I would fill out a form that helped us talk through what he was feeling and what was wrong. Then I would prompt him to "turn the crank," to mentally move on from the upsetting moment and rejoin the class.

One day Andrew's feelings were hurt by another boy in the class. So we processed what happened and filled out the form. I said, "Andrew, it's time to turn the crank."

He turned to me with tear-filled eyes. "I can't turn the crank on this one, Mrs. Mac."

Bless him. We can all relate. We all have times when life is hard and not how we thought it would be. Turning the crank to move forward feels impossible. Staying in the miserable stuck place appears to be the only option. Thankfully, I had "turned the crank" from my expectations of where I thought I'd be and decided to fill the space God had given me as a teacher's assistant.

Another part of my job was to accompany Andrew to his speech-language pathology sessions. During those sessions, God lit a fire in my heart. Each week I asked the SLP more questions about her job. More and more, I realized how perfectly the career aligned with my love of science, my desire to help others, my interest in working with kids, and my need for flexibility with my future family plans.

Around the same time I felt a pull to pursue further training to become an SLP, Bruce's job moved us to San Francisco. Another new city. Unlike with my move to Chicago, here absolutely nothing resembled my Midwest experience. Even the topography of San Fran's steep hills stood in stark contrast to the flatlands of my home state of Indiana.

Once again I found myself alone in a city with no direction. I had applied to an SLP graduate program but had not been accepted. The feelings of a "stranded nobody" surfaced again. But this time, based on my experience with the teacher's assistant job, I decided to consider my space and fill it. Instead of moping around and feeling sorry for myself, I volunteered at the hospital down the street from our apartment. During orientation they presented different volunteer positions. Wouldn't you know there was an opening to volunteer in the speech-language pathology department. *And* on my first day volunteering, the managing SLP offered me a job as an SLP assistant. Once again, God taught me how what seems like a step backward is actually a step into the purpose He has planned for me.

Since following the normal path hadn't worked for me and following God's leading had, I decided to go out on a limb and contact the university where I'd been rejected. Amazingly, they said I could audit classes as a local resident even if I wasn't officially in the program. (And bonus: It was cheaper than if I'd paid full tuition!)

Fast-forward one more year and Bruce decided to start his own hedge fund in Chicago. Because I had taken a year of undergrad prerequisites and worked as an SLP assistant, I applied and was accepted into Northwestern University's master's program, a top-three program. A year prior, I had been rejected by a state school for the same type of master's program. But by occupying my space, being willing to volunteer at the hospital, and making time to audit classes as an unofficial student, the next space God provided was an amazing experience in a well-respected graduate program. I didn't take one moment for granted while attending that program. I had seen God's hand work in my life, and I knew my part in His big story.

No More, No Less

Another Google result for *anavah* led me to a Jewish devotional on Moses. Numbers 12:3 has this parenthetical statement: "(Now Moses was a very humble man, more humble than anyone else on the face of the earth)" (NIV). Since Moses is credited with writing the book of Numbers, this statement is confusing. It doesn't seem very humble to call yourself more humble than any other person on the face of the earth. But what if we apply the expanded definition of *humility*? Then the passage could be read as, "Moses occupied his God-given space more than anyone else on the face of the earth." We can see how that is true.

The statement about humility comes after Moses's siblings question his role. "They said, 'Has the LORD spoken only through Moses? Has he not spoken through us also?' And the LORD heard it" (v. 2). They complain about Moses's seemingly bigger role. They feel less important, like stranded nobodies. Ultimately, they are questioning God's assignments.

The author of that Jewish devotional writes,

> We practice *anavah* when we fully occupy the space to which we are entitled as human beings created in the Divine image, neither under- nor over-stepping our proper boundaries: in Alan Morinis's now well-known phrase, "no more than our space, and no less than our place." We practice *anavah* when we are aware of being a precious part of an infinitely larger whole, and act in accordance with that awareness.[5]

While Miriam and Aaron are asking, "Hey, what about us? Don't we do what Moses does?" they are forgetting the divine invitation I wrote about in the last chapter. God assigned Moses to the leadership role. A role Moses was reluctant to accept from the beginning. Because another way the lie of insignificance can creep in is when the assigned space feels too large and we feel too small.

When God assigns Moses to go to Pharoah, Moses says, "Who am *I* . . . ?" (Exod. 3:11, emphasis added). God doesn't respond with, "Oh, you are so amazing, Moses. You've got this!" Instead, He reassures Moses with His presence and flips the question of "Who am I?" with a reminder of who God is: "I AM WHO I AM" (v. 14).

When the assigned space feels too large and we feel too small, we are forgetting that the Creator God assigned us. And no space is too large for Him and no assignment too hard. Like I said before, we miss the bigger plan in place.

We also forget that the results are not our responsibility.

I remember sitting in our final spring Mothers of Preschoolers (MOPS) meeting. Having been up since 4:00 a.m. to watch the royal wedding with my mentor and friends, my brain was a bit foggy. But I'd been asked to give a testimony of how MOPS supported my mom journey. Even though I had taken time to plan what I would say, as I sat there listening to the other moms' testimonies, my words felt less needed. Hadn't they already covered everything? I turned to my friend Misty and whispered, "I don't think I need to share anymore. I don't have anything to add."

She kindly disagreed. "Yes, you do! These women need to hear what you have to say. Get up there and share!"

The space of speaking was intimidating for me. My ability to contribute or perform felt too small.

But God.

While I was up in front of my friends sharing my story, new ideas came together and spilled out of my mouth. I shared how I had tried to be a child-centered mom and then had swung to being a self-centered one out of exhaustion before finally landing in the freedom and grace of being a God-centered mom. Right there in the space I'd been invited but reluctant to fill, God gave me my first online assignment: GodCenteredMom.com. A site where I could write about the daily process of focusing on God instead of idolizing my kids or my comfort. An ironic thing given that—like I shared at the start of the chapter—I didn't prefer writing. Here God directed me to a space to write out words . . . for His glory. That's the key.

When I was homeschooled, it once took me two months to write an essay. Not because I couldn't but because I didn't want to sit down and do the work. My mom was at her wit's end trying to motivate me. Finally, she threatened not to let me participate in my next synchronized swimming meet. I guess that was the boundary I needed in order to know she was serious. And it was time to stop running from something that I needed to do but found challenging.

Like when a literary agent reached out to me a year after I started writing online. He sent me an email asking if I'd ever considered book publishing. The answer was no. Especially since he emailed me a month after my fourth son was born, when my oldest was six. After emailing back and forth with him, I remembered that a good college friend worked in the publishing industry. So I called her and asked what she thought about me writing a book.

First she said, "Heather! This is a big deal. I'm editing two of his clients' books right now. What an amazing opportunity!" Then she went on to say, "I'm wondering if perhaps this isn't the best time to work on a book. What would it look like if you waited five years?" She might as well have said wait a billion years. Remember what I said in the last chapter about my FOMO struggles? Waiting felt like missing out. Stepping away from this opportunity felt foolish. Don't people work for years to get the chance to talk to a literary agent? And I had one reaching out to me!

So I ignored her wise advice and pushed forward working on a book proposal. To give myself focused writing time, I hired a babysitter to watch the boys at home, and I would often go to Panera and write for chunks of time. One day, I was working and two friends came in to have lunch together just feet away from my table. Instead of tapping away at my keyboard, I desperately wanted to pull up a chair and join their conversation. With rare kid-free time during the day, missing out on time with my gal pals felt like a gut punch. How do I keep writing while I witness them laugh, nod, and connect? In that moment, book writing felt like a sacrificial space. Choosing to work on it meant not being with my boys and not socializing with friends. But all the sacrifice was worth it because I was occupying the space God assigned to me. Right?

I'll never forget the first phone call with my agent to discuss the rough draft. He started the conversation with, "How long did you work on this?"

Uh, how do I answer that question? If I say, "Not that long," it may appear I don't care. But if he hated it and I say I worked a long time on it, then it shows weak skills. I landed on "I worked on it for a while." That felt vague enough to satisfy his inquiry.

Then he went on to say words that are etched in my memory: "You write like a fifty-year-old woman." That was interesting because at the time my sister was fifty years old, and they say your family is the age of your oldest child. Maybe, given the structure of my family of origin, I write as though I'm the age of my oldest sister.

Then he said, "You aren't the female James Dobson. You can't just jump into teaching as if you have authority." Okayyy. Loud and clear. So, not only had I sacrificed to be in this space but now I was failing at filling it.

I thought I was being obedient. I thought I had heard God correctly and was following his direction. But after that conversation, I closed my laptop and decided I would never write again and that I would rather go get my nails done. On the way to the salon, I called Bruce. I shed a few tears while updating him on the agent's feedback. I also told him about my decision to no longer write a book because it was harder than I thought it would be. He gently suggested that perhaps, like other creative endeavors, the process would take time and several rough drafts to refine my skills. Maybe he was right.

After a fresh pedicure and some perspective, I decided to try working on a book proposal again. Although it would be another ten years before I published my first book (more on that later), I learned that just because something is hard doesn't mean I heard God wrong. Sometimes an assignment is harder when we try to succeed on our own.

Kind of like Moses dealing with grumbling followers. He's done what God has asked. He's led the people where they need to go. But the satisfaction rating of the Israelites is two stars. Food is literally falling from the sky, but they prefer a little more diet variety. They complain that they'd rather be slaves in Egypt than in their current situation. So Moses cries out to God about feeding all the people (as a mom of four boys I can relate): "Where am I to get meat to give to all this people? For they come weeping to me, saying, 'Give us meat to eat!' I am not able to carry all this people alone, for they are too heavy for me" (Num. 11:13–14). He's right.

Although God has assigned him to the space of leading the Israelites, Moses is a limited human, and what is required of him is beyond his abilities. He needs boundaries. Clarity on what is his space to fill and what isn't. In admitting his lack, Moses is instructed by God to gather seventy men to help him lead the people. Seventy! Moses has to recognize what is his part, what is God's part, and what is someone else's job to do.

Draw the Lines

A big part of occupying your God-given space is defining the boundaries of your space. What is yours to fill and what isn't? "No more than our space, no less than our place." When considering drawing boundaries, I think about the story in Joshua 15 (hat tip to my friend Joel for sharing with me after painstakingly reading that portion of Scripture during his one-year Bible challenge). Although a bit tedious to read, this passage defines each boundary line for the territory of Judah, the space God instructed the Israelites to occupy, a.k.a. the promised land.

What would these boundary lines look like for our spaces? I think they would include these four distinct elements that we will explore further in the coming chapters:

1. Time—your position in this moment in history
2. Place—your physical environment
3. Wiring—your unique personality, interests, and gifts
4. Experiences—your challenges and joys

Sometimes occupying our spaces looks like a great success and sometimes it feels like death—both fit in our expanded definition of *humility*. Thankfully, Jesus modeled this by going first: "He humbled himself and became obedient to the point of death—even death on a cross" (Phil. 2:8). Jesus submitted to God's will by hanging on the cross. That act of trusting God's greater plan led to the world's salvation—true success.

> Therefore God exalted him even more highly
>> and gave him the name
>> that is above every other name,
> so that at the name given to Jesus
>> every knee should bend,
>> in heaven and on earth and under the earth,
> and every tongue should confess
>> that Jesus Christ is Lord,
>> to the glory of God the Father. (vv. 9–11)

Even though Christ, as God, knows He will be resurrected and exalted, He sits in a garden on the Mount of Olives and cries, "Father, if you are willing, remove this cup from me, yet not my will but yours be done" (Luke 22:42). He acknowledges His grief in the place God is assigning Him, but Jesus surrenders to God's ultimate will and purposes. In some versions of the Bible, after this prayer, an angel attends to Jesus and gives Him strength.

It was my friend Jenn ("stranded nobody") who helped me see the truth of who God can be in your humbling circumstances. One day, in the midst of one of the hardest spaces I've been assigned, she brought me a small gift: the booklet called *The Red Sea Rules*. It was the exact copy that had been given to her by a mentor seven years before at a time when Jenn had been hospitalized and we almost lost her. Not only did the author of this little book provide encouragement, the penciled-in Scripture and underlined words from previous owners reminded me I wasn't the first to be stuck in undesirable circumstances. Others have made it to the other side of suffering.

I was reminded of the miraculous things God can do when we are assigned an impossible space, like Moses and the Israelites between the Egyptian army and the Red Sea. When we feel hopeless,

God sees a third option. He splits the sea and leads us to His next assignment. God will make a way. Maybe not the way we desire, but He will make a way where there was no apparent way. In the words of author and pastor Robert Morgan, "The same God who led you in will lead you out."[6]

Did you notice how Jenn, the one who believed herself to be a "nobody," became my "everybody" in the right moment? Sense of purpose is relative. If we look to the culture to define success, we'll come up short. It's all about filling the space God has appointed you to. In doing so, you discover the humble success of being right where you belong. Whether we're staying home teaching and caring for kids, working as an emergency-room physician, or handing a hurting friend a meaningful book, the most humble thing we can do is take up just the right amount of space.

DISCUSSION QUESTIONS

1. Consider a season when you felt unimportant and not successful. How did you respond to that feeling?
2. How would you have defined *humility* before reading this chapter?
3. How are you encouraged by the expanded version of *humility*: "to occupy your God-given space"?
4. When was a time you were assigned a space that felt too big for you?
5. How have others' responses caused you to question if you are in the wrong role/position/place?

IDENTIFY YOUR GOD-GIVEN SPACE

In the next four chapters, we will work through identifying the boundary lines of your God-given space. The goal is to articulate where you are physically or metaphorically placed. Through examples and questions, you'll begin to recognize your reality as good and right, even if it doesn't follow the pattern of your peers or the idealized story you imagined for yourself.

Boundary Line of Time

"I wish it need not have happened in my time," said Frodo. "So do I," said Gandalf, "and so do all who live to see such times. But that is not for them to decide. All we have to decide is what to do with the time that is given us."

J. R. R. Tolkien, *Fellowship of the Ring*

All my days were written in your book and planned before a single one of them began.

Psalm 139:16 CSB

I n high school, we read a book called *Flatland*.[1] The main character is "a Square," who writes from prison, having been arrested for trying to educate others on the third dimension. He encounters "the Stranger," a sphere from Spaceland who is visiting Flatland, attempting to enlighten others about a third dimension. Can you picture the meeting? A two-dimensional square in a conversation with a three-dimensional sphere. The Square describes the Stranger entering Flatland as a small dot growing into a larger and larger circle, shrinking again, and finally completely disappearing. The Square has only two-dimensional vocabulary to describe a three-dimensional object.

I'm sure most of us can relate to the Square. You and I struggle to have words to describe the fourth dimension of time. Remember the movie *Back to the Future*? The title itself is confusing. To add to the confusion, mathematicians continue to prove more dimensions exist. I think they have discovered at least ten. Ten dimensions! And we can barely grasp a fourth. But not only did God create all of them, He has access to each one. The study of multidimensionality increases my faith. It reminds me of my finite ability to understand an infinite, multidimensional God.

In the Bible we read that God is not bound by time since He is eternal in both directions of our concept of time. That means God looks at the whole of your life, from conception in the womb to your last breath on earth, and He sees it all at once. Like when I hold a pen in my hand, I can see the whole pen and all around the pen at the same time. This is how God sees the entirety of your time here on earth—a minuscule blip on the eternal timeline. That's perhaps why Solomon writes in Ecclesiastes about the vanity of life, or it's meaninglessness. But the Hebrew word Solomon uses is *hevel*, and a better translation than "meaningless" is "vapor" or "smoke."[2] Existing for a very small moment, like smoke or vapor. Another reminder to stay humble in this God-given space in all eternity.

Just like multidimensionality is based on string theory (don't ask me to explain it though), our lives are knit, or strung together, by a series of events orchestrated by the Master Creator. Although your parents may have been surprised by your conception, God was not. In fact, my God-given vapor moment started because of a psych intern and a failed IUD.

Let me explain.

Sixteen years before I came on the scene, my mom was pregnant at sixteen years old with my sister. As was common at the time with teen pregnancies, my grandparents planned to fly my mom to Arizona, where she would spend the last part of her pregnancy, and then place my sister for adoption. Afterward my mom would return to Indiana and complete her high school degree. But my parents had other plans.

One day immediately after school, a friend picked up my mom and drove her and my dad to the airport. They flew to Kentucky, where they planned to lie about my mom's age and elope. All was going according to plan until the courthouse judge got a call from my grandparents.

Apparently, my parents' airport ride snitched. And when my grandparents learned about the marriage plans, they started calling every courthouse in Louisville. Once they located my parents, they told the judge to put my mom in foster care (since she was under eighteen) and my dad in prison (since he was twenty at the time). *Gulp.*

After coordinating care for their other children, my grandparents made the drive down to Kentucky. When they arrived at the foster care facility, a staff member (who they presumed was a doctor) counseled them and convinced them to allow my parents to get married. Oh to have been a fly on the wall for that conversation! What words did he weave together to change their hearts? I wish I had them etched in stone. Or maybe cross-stitched on a pillow. This man, who they later discovered was a humble psych intern, changed my life. Or, I should say, he helped string together the events that led to my life. Most likely he never got an update about how that sixteen-year-old and twenty-year-old stayed married for fifty-five years. Or how that baby in my mom's womb would one day adopt a little boy who was conceived by another teen mom. The ripple effects of one conversation in time are mind-boggling.

Fast-forward to the time of my conception. My mom and dad had two children: my sixteen-year-old sister and my eleven-year-old brother. As you can imagine, life was a whole lot easier for them having older children. In fact, my mom had been leading Bible studies and teaching at women's events. She was asked to join an exclusive speaking team for women's retreats, a rare opportunity for women of faith at the time. Unfortunately, that invitation came the same day she learned about being pregnant with me. What was most shocking was that she had an IUD, which is designed to prohibit an egg from implanting in the uterine lining. But where there's a will, there's a way. And God knit my life right into that womb despite a device telling Him otherwise.

Have you considered the string of events that came together for your life to exist? How did your parents meet? If you've been told you were an "accident" or a "mistake," I would beg to differ. Like I said earlier, we struggle to conceptualize beyond our three dimensions. One way we can occupy our God-given space is to believe there is no mistake or accident when God decides to place us at this moment in time. Even if you never know the purpose, the connection between your existence and what God is working together for His bigger plan matters more than your understanding.

Where Were You?

When I consider questioning whether God got it wrong in giving me this life, particularly when life is hard, I think of the book of Job, where we find the story of a man who loves God and lives a successful life. Then tragedy strikes repeatedly: the loss of his family, his wealth, his home, and even his physical health. At his lowest point, after poor comfort from his friends and his wife's suggestion to "curse [or bless] God and die" (Job 2:9), he questions God: "Why did I not die at birth, come forth from the womb and expire?" (3:11). He believes all of his pain and suffering could have been avoided if God had not given him life. To emphasize his desire, he continues his lament to God: "Why did you bring me forth from the womb? Would that I had died before any eye had seen me" (10:18).

God listens to Job's words. He can handle anger and wrestling. But He "rightsizes" Job by answering his questions with more questions:

> *Where were you* when I laid the foundation of the earth?
>   Tell me, if you have understanding.
> *Who* determined its measurements—*surely you know!*
>   Or who stretched the line upon it?
> On what were its bases sunk,
>   or who laid its cornerstone? (38:4–6, emphasis added)

He continues for several chapters, asking Job if he knows the "why" behind various aspects of creation. Can he explain God's creation to God? The last chapter of Job is labeled "Job Is Humbled and Satisfied." If we apply our definition of *humility*, it could read, "Job Is Fully Occupying His God-Given Space and Is Satisfied." *Before* his health, wealth, and family are restored, Job recognizes God's sovereignty:

> I know that you can do all things
>   and that no purpose of yours can be thwarted. . . .
> Therefore I have uttered what I did not understand,
>   things too wonderful for me that I did not know.
>   (42:2–3)

When my mom discovered she was pregnant with me, she could have questioned God: *Why are You disrupting my life with a new baby? Why are You assigning me to the new-mom space when I thought I was moving into a new season of my career? This is not how I saw my life going.* Maybe she asked those questions, I don't know. Perhaps in your timeline, you've questioned why God allowed something to happen at an inopportune time or not in the time frame you would have preferred. You've sought out every expert for physical healing. You've been waiting to find a husband. You've been trying to have a child. You've been hit with wave after wave of suffering.

You've stalled out, waiting for your dream to become a reality. In seasons of suffering, time stands still.

We throw around the phrases, "everything in its season," "this is a hard season," and "it's only for a season." We even quote another section from Ecclesiastes (or from the Byrds song): "For everything there is a season, and a time for every matter under heaven: a time to be born, and a time to die" (3:1–2 ESV). Sometimes our hearts plead for a different season. In the dreariness of winter, we long for the joy of spring.

I've witnessed what can happen when nature doesn't follow the assigned seasons. One fall while I was visiting Pennsylvania, a snowstorm blew in and dropped twelve inches of snow. While that amount wasn't unusual for the community, having that much snow arrive while leaves still hung on the trees was. I had never considered the importance of trees losing their leaves before snow falls. The leaves became receptacles for accumulating snow, and the weight of gathering snow caused the limbs to snap. The ripple effect of trees losing branches was catastrophic: crushing cars, taking down power lines, and blocking roads. All because one season arrived too early.

One aspect of occupying our God-given spaces is to trust that no matter the current season, there are reasons we haven't moved on to the next one yet. Pruning, or loss, is painful but may be keeping us from burdens that could lead us to snap. While we move through chronological time, we learn to trust God's timing. Plans can be made and held loosely, not knowing what the next day holds.

As a senior in college, I decided to take a personal finance class from Bruce's favorite professor, Rick Seaman, even though I was a biology major. After significant success in business, Rick retired at the age of thirty-five. In his retirement, he chose to spend time with his family and teach business at Taylor University. His class was incredibly practical and helped me understand Bruce's interests more. The last week of class, Rick took us on a field trip to a funeral home. He didn't want us to be surprised by the cost when someone passes away. After the tour (which included an education I won't forget on embalming), he encouraged us to write up a plan so our families wouldn't have to deal with those details in their grief.

Right before we left, the funeral director looked at Rick and said, "You know, year after year you bring students in here, but you haven't created your plan with me yet." To which Rick responded, "You're absolutely right. I'll come back next Wednesday and we'll talk."

That Friday in class, Rick passed around a bag of candy and asked us to each take a piece while he gave us the final course lecture. In it, he reminded us of how God placed each of us on this earth for a purpose: "When God decides you have completed what He assigned you to do, He decides when it is your time to come back and be with Him."

Those words flooded back to my mind just two days later. While playing basketball with his son, Rick had a massive heart attack and passed away immediately. The following Wednesday, I found myself once again in that funeral home. This time it was to offer my condolences to his family. His passing didn't make earthly sense. Despite the fact that he had lived a full life in his forty-two years, we believe everyone deserves a long, happy life. We can sometimes wrongly assume everyone is guaranteed at least eighty years.

One day in November 2016, my mom called from Costa Rica to tell me she'd found a lump in her breast. Since her doctors were based in Dallas, my parents decided to come stay with us while my mom figured out next steps. We soon learned she had triple-negative breast cancer, and intensive chemotherapy needed to start immediately. After one round of her treatment, my dad started to get sick. When I arrived home one day, my dad greeted me, and his skin glowed yellow. A scan the next week revealed liver cancer, metastasized from a prior colon cancer diagnosis. He lived one more month after that day and passed away right before his seventy-sixth birthday.

The evening after we watched him take his last breath, my mom turned to me and said, "How do you go on living after fifty-five years of marriage?" I was reminded of something my mom had shared with me a few weeks earlier. While trying to decide whether she would go forward with chemotherapy, she had read a story in 2 Kings. In the story, Hezekiah is sick, and Isaiah warns him to get his affairs in order because he is about to die. Instead of listening to Isaiah's instructions, Hezekiah pleads for his life. Before Isaiah even leaves the court, he hears from the Lord:

> Turn back, and say to Hezekiah the leader of my people, Thus says the LORD, the God of David your father: I have heard your prayer; I have seen your tears. Behold, I will heal you. . . . I will add fifteen years to your life. (20:5–6 ESV)

My mom felt that the Lord was promising her healing and fifteen more years of life if she pursued treatment.

Considering all she'd lost in a short time—her health, her home in Costa Rica, and her husband—she was at a place of suffering like Job. The person who sat with her, processing the pain, was me, the daughter who entered the earth as a surprise. And forty years after my birth, I encouraged her with these words: "Mom, you lived sixteen years before marrying dad. You believe God has promised you fifteen more years of life. Those are your bookends. Your ministry has not ended because of dad's passing." You better believe she has embraced every bit of this bookended life. She teaches Bible studies, guides preschoolers through the Awana discipleship program, and leads children to Christ in her Good News Club.

We can make plans for the future, but God knows the number of our days. It's rare to get a promise about that number, like Hezekiah did or like my mom believes she did. We don't know the length of time we're allocated on earth to fulfill our various assignments. The key is to see where we are in time and steward the present moment.

Unwrap the Present

Beyond trusting God with our moment in history and the timing of our seasons, there is really only one assigned space in time that we control. That is our response in the present moment. Whether you're wired to dwell on the past or plan for the future, both of those mental exercises happen in the present moment. The only way to impact the future is in how we handle what's right in front of us.

In Scripture we read about God giving supernatural insight about the future. He divinely inspires the prophets to speak warnings, visions, and future events. Unless God has given us that glimpse into the future, we can see only what's right in front of us. In the book *The Sacrament of the Present Moment*, Jean-Pierre de Caussade writes, "What (God) ordains for us each moment is what is most holy, best, and most divine. All we need to know is how to recognize his will in the present moment."[3] A pure desire but difficult to execute.

There are so many possibilities for how we can spend each moment of our time. So many resources exist on time management. I am constantly challenged by wanting to do more to help friends, neighbors, or family but finding the tyranny of the urgent (dishes, laundry, email, carpool) taking up the majority of my minutes. When my kids were younger, my mind would scroll through the questions, *Do I clean the house? Do I play with the boys? Do I create something? Do I rest and read?* And most often I ended up scrolling on my phone, numbing out from having to choose.

Once, I shared with my friend Nancy about how I felt I was failing my friends. Occupied with caring for my boys, our home, Bruce, and my job, I wasn't as intentional as I would've liked to have been in reaching out to check on people. Nancy comforted me with the words, "If God brings someone to mind, reach out to them. Otherwise release the burden that you need to spend your time doing that."

What Nancy suggested is similar to what de Caussade writes

as a prayer to guide us moment to moment: "'Lord, what should I do?' Let me do everything you wish. The Spirit wants one thing, the body another, but Lord, I wish only to do your divine will."[4]

My friend Robin shared with me that his acronym for the year is WIN, which stands for "What's Important Now." Any time he's conflicted about how to spend his time or energy, he asks himself that clarifying question. It feels a bit idealistic to pray at all times for guidance, but what if you tried to do so in times when you are unsure how to spend the next moment? Or when you are with someone, pray, "Lord, focus my heart and mind on what's happening right here."

How often do we waste the present moment feeling regret for past failures or fear about future unknowns? If you and I fully occupy our God-given space in the present moment, then instead of judging our former selves when we reflect on the past, we can respond with grace that we did the best we could do at that time. And instead of fearing future realities, we can focus mental energy on right now. As author, speaker, and mentor Vicki Kraft says, "There's no grace for your imagination."[5] Grace exists in the present. When challenges arise, God will meet you there and lead you through.

After my first failed attempt at a book proposal, I wondered if perhaps this "opportunity" was actually a distraction from my primary assignment to take care of my four boys. Was I neglecting the role of discipleship in my home by working on the book? On the other hand, what if writing was God's invitation, and it wasn't about choosing between the two assignments but about being more creative with time management? How long did I spend on Facebook or reading friends' blogs (remember this was 2012)? Did I need to binge-watch that TV show at night? What if I woke up early and worked on the book? Of course, I discovered there was plenty of margin for me to occupy the space of writing a book proposal that wouldn't take away from parenting my boys.

In those nooks and crannies, I finished the proposal just in time for a writers' conference. My agent had scheduled a meeting with me, and I was under the impression we would talk with publishers about the book. I showed up to the conference and realized something was off. My author friends had brought multiple copies of their proposals and scheduled several different publisher meetings. I had one copy and one meeting in the hotel lobby. Slightly distracted by the football game on the big-screen TV, my agent let me know that he didn't think there was a market for a mom book anymore. He explained that lots of mommy bloggers had signed book contracts over the past year, and publishers weren't extending mom-book contracts right now. *Gut punch.* Why would God provide an opportunity, lead me to put time and energy into working on the project, and then leave me empty-handed?

A few hours before my meeting, I'd heard Bianca Olthoff teach on the Valley of Dry Bones (see Ezek. 37). She'd shared about how God brought the prophet Ezekiel to a valley full of bones and asked him to prophesy life over the bones. Ezekiel obeyed and the bones and muscles gathered together. Then God breathed life into the bodies.

While I was sitting in that hotel lobby, my plans for writing a book felt like a pile of dry bones. In that moment, I decided I didn't want to pursue anything until God decided to breathe life into it. Having cleared my calendar of commitments thinking I would be writing a book, I had time on my hands.

I'd heard about podcasting from a few of my friends in the blogging world. In 2013, with the help of my friends Katie Orr and Kat Lee, I decided to use my newfound time to start a podcast called *God Centered Mom.* In a time when not many podcasts existed, I had no idea where that small decision would lead me. Following God's lead in the present moment paved a way for a future I could have never planned or orchestrated.

For Such a Time as This

We talk about God's timing being perfect—it may not be perfect for us. Have you considered why God waited as long as He did for the Messiah, Jesus, to be born? Why didn't Jesus come as David's grandson? Why not a child of Adam and Eve? The Israelites' journey to the promised land should have taken months, not forty years. Their exile in Babylon lasted seventy years. The Lord was silent for five hundred years between the Old and New Testaments. Then a teenage girl supernaturally gets pregnant at the time of Roman rule. Why?

Jesus arrived at the perfect time. Galatians 4:4–5 says, "But when the fullness of time had come, God sent his Son, born of a woman, born under the law, in order to redeem those who were under the law, so that we might receive adoption as children." According to author Don Stewart, when Jesus came, "there was an international language that all the citizens of the empires spoke, Greek. There was peace in the empire and a great road system that made travel easy. Ultimately, however, the reason for that particular time in history for Jesus to come into the world is known to God alone."[6]

While you want to believe God's timing is perfect, sometimes you might dismiss an assignment thinking your time has passed. Let me introduce you to my friend Kim Cash Tate. After establishing her career as a lawyer, Kim felt God leading her to stay home full-time with her kids and homeschool them. That decision to follow God in the space He had assigned her took her places she could have never imagined. She later became a fiction and devotional writer. And with her children fully grown, she recently created and stars in a web series with over one hundred thousand YouTube subscribers. At fifty years old, she performs in music videos from the show's soundtrack. Kim's goal has always been to cling to God and follow His lead in her life.

Recently, I saw a post from Kim on Instagram encouraging older women to pursue what God is assigning them:

You felt the nudge, but you're like, "This doesn't make sense at all at my age. That's for younger people." Sorta like having babies? Because clearly God could have found somebody younger when he

60

wanted to call a people to himself. He said, "I'm gonna choose a seventy-five-year-old. Then I'm gonna wait until he turns a hundred and his wife is ninety before she gives birth." . . . When time came for John the Baptist to come into the world, God said, "I'm gonna choose two people so old the angels gonna have to rebuke the daddy because he can't believe it could be true. Sure enough, Elizabeth got pregnant. . . . So you tell Elizabeth and Sarah you're too old to carry out the plan and purpose of God. Stop depriving God of the opportunity to get the glory and show himself strong through you.[7]

Those last words are crucial when considering your space to occupy. In looking at the boundary line of time, don't put a limit on God's ability to use you on His timeline.

There is an ordering to the minutes in our days. The Greek word often used is *chronos*. Another word used in the New Testament for time is *kairos*, and it can mean "the appointed time in the purpose of God," the time when God acts.[8] This is when the mundane moments—our given space to occupy—transform into divine appointments. Our role is to trust He is at work in *kairos* time as we fill the *chronos* time. Perhaps the Holy Spirit will give us glimpses into what God is doing and how.

In Acts 1, the disciples ask Jesus, "Lord, will you *at this time* restore the kingdom to Israel?" (v. 6 ESV, emphasis added). They hope to see the Israelite kingdom return in their lifetime. But God is up to so much more than they could have imagined. Jesus responds with, "It is not for you to know times or seasons that the Father has fixed by his own authority. But you will receive power when the Holy Spirit has come upon you, and you will be my witnesses in Jerusalem and in all Judea and Samaria, and to the end of the earth" (vv. 7–8 ESV).

Jesus gives them their divine assignments: They are empowered by the Spirit to be witnesses of the gospel. The disciples' martyrdom is not glamorous. They do not see the gospel move across the globe. They are faithful to fill the time they have been given.

Like God promises Ezekiel with that valley of dry bones, "I will put my Spirit within you, and you shall live, and I will place you in your own land" (37:14 ESV). Followers of Jesus have been filled with His Spirit to live in the places He assigns us.

The first boundary line of your God-given space is time. By considering your spot on the *chronos* timeline, your current season, and even your present moment, you can be comforted. You aren't too young, too old, too late, or too early to follow God's invitations. Surrendering to the Spirit's leading in daily choices adds up to a life well lived. In fact, I know God appointed you *for such a time as this* (see Esther 4:14) in His larger redemptive story. You belong right here, right now.

DISCUSSION QUESTIONS

1. What events did God string together to bring you into this world? Consider your parents' and grandparents' stories. Even if your life began in challenging circumstances, consider taking a moment to say a prayer of gratitude to God for giving you life.

2. How does knowing that God sees the whole of your life at once change how you live your life today?

3. Think of a difficult time in your life. Reflect back on that hard season. What have you gained or learned? How did you see God's perfect timing at work?

4. Do you struggle with thinking too much about how you spent your time in the past or worrying about the future?

5. How does knowing that your present moment is the space God is asking you to fill change how you spend your time now?

Boundary Line of Place

As long as there are people, Christ will walk the earth as your neighbor, as the one through whom God calls you, speaks to you, makes demands on you.

Christ is standing at the door; he lives in the form of a human being among us.

Do you want to close the door or open it?

Dietrich Bonhoeffer

My grandfather was born in a log cabin. Take a moment to let that sink in. A log cabin. I am not making this up. I watched hours of *Little House on the Prairie*, and never once did I consider that my grandpa lived a similar life.

Recently I was going through some files and found a twenty-page document titled "A Few Memories from the Life of Cecil Ralph Price." What struck me was how in 2022 we publicly post the mundane details of life, like our morning fancy-foam-art-topped latte. Yet in a short booklet that lay forgotten in a desk drawer, my grandfather had written out the high and low points of his entire life. Including a couple brief sentences about the losses of his first wife to cancer and his second wife to a stroke.

During the Depression, my grandfather made $1.25 a day for shoveling gravel for nine hours. Over and over throughout the booklet, he shares his attempts at "striking it rich"—purchasing oil fields, inventing his own home freezer, printing fifty thousand social security tags. About to purchase 950 miles of pipeline in Nebraska, he writes, "Just before the final papers were signed one of the key people lost his life in a gas pumping house explosion. It was a little tough for this country boy to see his dreams of becoming a millionaire evaporate."

When I was growing up, we would visit my grandfather in his mobile home, a reality that his millionaire dreams never came true. From a child's perspective, the significance of where he lived didn't change how I saw him or the value I placed on his role in my life. Although that country boy never saw his dreams realized, a few beautiful threads were woven throughout his story. God kept directing him to work at different print shops. And one day, he took a risk and bought his own shop, the Price Printing Company, at 33 Virginia Avenue in downtown Indianapolis.

I also noticed a few writing samples he'd slipped in with the memoir. One of those samples was a hilarious letter in which he expresses his concerns about his pastor's desire to destroy moles in the area. "If there were no more moles, where would Dr. Scholl's foot comfort people get the raw material that make the foot pads, corn pads, bunion pads, etc. that are made from 'Mole-Skin'?" He proceeds to offer a few suggestions if the pastor insists on destroying the "non-violent, bashful, little creatures" and concludes with an apparently random aside: "I expect that by now you have heard John is campaigning for US Congress in the new Sixth District." John is my dad.

So, despite the loss of his millionaire dreams, this country boy with only a high school diploma managed to own his own business and rear a child who pursued a law degree and ran for several political offices. My grandfather didn't choose to be born in a humble log cabin. He tried as hard as he could to make his way in the world and prove that he mattered. He'll never see the global ripple effect of faithfully occupying his God-given space. Or that his story has been retold in a book written by his granddaughter.

Like my grandfather, you didn't choose where your life began or how you ended up on that piece of the planet. Neither the timing of your life nor where it began was a surprise to God. Yet both play an important role in defining your space today.

Cozy Garden Life

If you've ever been apartment hunting in a big city like Chicago or New York, you understand how unique one unit is from another. It's not like going to a rental center saying you want a two-bedroom apartment and the agent showing you three possible floor plans. With urban living, each unit is managed separately and has its own quirks.

Back in 2001 when we were looking for an apartment in Chicago, there weren't even fancy websites to help make the job easier. We scanned through magazine listings for something that matched our needs. After a few days of seeing places firsthand, we became savvier in knowing what certain descriptors actually meant. For example, *cozy* always meant "small." And *garden apartment* sounds lovely until you see your first one and realize that it actually means "below garden level" (a.k.a. basement dwelling). Then there was the apartment listing that highlighted the convenience of being close to the elevated train ("the el") but failed to mention that the tracks literally ran outside the second-story apartment's windows. Or that a bustling bar occupied the first floor of the building.

Something inside of us longs for a peaceful, comfortable place to dwell. I think it's a bit of our souls longing to get back to the Garden (very different from the garden apartment). In the beginning, God made humans in His image and created a perfect place for them to dwell, where all their needs were met. Adam and Eve held dominion over the Garden. Then everything changed. Desmond Alexander writes, "By heeding the serpent they not only give it control over the earth, but they themselves become its subjects."[1] Because of sin, the world we live in is not the shalom place God created it to be. Barry Jones says, "God's glorious intention for his good creation is subverted. The wholeness and harmony we were created to enjoy with God, with each other, with creation and with ourselves is fundamentally violated."[2] Neal Plantinga defines sin as "the vandalism of shalom."[3]

The reason our places consistently fall short of our Garden ideals is because they are vandalized by the realities of evil. You will not find lasting contentment, comfort, or even coziness in any physical environment until all things are restored to shalom at the end of time. Even on the perfect, all-inclusive Mexican beach vacation you will find some discomforts, something to critique as being "off." The unsettled feeling you have in the location in which you find yourself ought to be expected. Moving to a new place will not bring the shalom you seek.

That concept doesn't apply just to a physical place but also to a perceived place of power or significance. Sometimes I see a group of influencers on social media and want to be in their position. I want the invitation to what seems like a better place. Perhaps *there* I will finally matter. Which reminds me of the story of Damocles.

Damocles believes life will be better in the palace. So he flatters King Dionysius, telling him how lucky he is to be a man of power and authority in a place surrounded by luxuries. In response, the king offers to switch places with Damocles so he can experience life on the throne. Damocles does not skip a beat in accepting the invitation. He finds himself surrounded by beautiful rugs, an array of lavish foods, piles of silver and gold, and staff at his disposal. But Dionysius includes something else in Damocles's experience.

Because of the many enemies the king has made during his reign, Dionysius "arranged that a sword should hang above the throne, held at the pommel only by a single hair of a horse's tail to evoke the sense of what it is like to be king: though having much fortune, always having to watch in fear and anxiety against dangers that might try to overtake him."[4] The pressure is too much for Damocles. He begs the king for permission to leave the palace. He realizes, while glamorous and fortunate, the responsibility that accompanies such power is too much to bear.

There have been times I've envied those in places of power, modern-day thrones, but have come to the same conclusion as Damocles. It is God's grace to gradually give me more responsibility and power—at the rate and pace my soul can bear. God's placement of us in our current location is not accidental or meaningless. It doesn't mean we won't move from one place to another. We will talk about that process later. But one question to consider when it comes to the boundary line of place is, What is my heart's posture toward my current physical place?

Divine Platform

When we moved from downtown Chicago to Dallas, we were accustomed to what I call "living amongst the people," in an environment where everyone walked along streets lined with fun shops and restaurants. When we bought our first home, during our pre-kid life, we didn't look at the school districts or whether kids played in the front yards. Instead, we positioned ourselves within walking distance of restaurants and shops.

As we started to have kids, we began to question our decision. Being one block from the highway was convenient but maybe not the safest for letting kids play in the front yard (especially since our street led directly to the highway on-ramp). Absolutely none of our neighbors had young children to play with our kids. The public school our property fed into had classes up to only the third grade.

Choosing to embrace our neighborhood, I took my young boys on nature walks up and down the block most days after nap time.

Just four houses down from ours, we would stop and say hello to Miss Sue and greet whatever rescue dog lived with her at the time. With each conversation we learned a bit more of Miss Sue's story. How she'd raised three boys into manhood. And how she'd lived alone for over a decade until her sister Kate moved into the small house on the back of her property.

When we met Miss Kate for the first time, she said, "Sue mentioned y'all go to church, where do you go?" Now, I had never once mentioned to Sue that we went to church. Yet somehow in living our lives and coming in contact with Sue, she had drawn the correct conclusion. Kate shared with me how she had been praying for Sue's salvation for years. So she celebrated when she heard that our family's life had intersected with Sue's.

Speaking of our church, we have a mission statement: "By 2026 we will be having thousands of easy-to-start conversations around the city. Because we believe that where God has us is where Jesus is." This goes back to what I said in chapter 1. God's presence is no longer confined to a cloud or a tabernacle or a temple. But because of Christ's death and resurrection, we are promised God's presence will dwell in us.

The Hebrew word for tabernacle is *mishkan*, which means "dwelling place."[5] You've heard people say the body is the temple of God. This space, your physical being, is the God-given space you've been assigned. Over the course of your lifetime, wherever your body goes, God's presence travels with you. It's what our church calls your "divine platform." In your home, at your workplace, chatting with your cashier, on a bench at the park, you are positioned to bring the good news of Jesus wherever your two feet take you.

In 2021, we were prepping our house to sell it. Since our oldest son was about to get his driver's license, we thought moving closer to his high school would reduce the risk of something harmful happening to him. (It's hard enough for an experienced driver to navigate Dallas highways.) At the same time, I was working to launch my first book, *Don't Mom Alone*. We looked at so many different homes, and before we could put in an offer, they would be gone (a mix of a hot market, low inventory, and lots of people moving to Texas). It became clear that perhaps moving wasn't going to happen.

After a bit of disappointment, I realized that in the previous three years we'd had five different young families move within a block of our home. Parents gathered in the front yards while children ran and played. It was exactly what we'd hoped for when we moved in eighteen years before. I was hosting a podcast encouraging women not to mom alone and had a new book about to release on the same topic. Once we decided not to move, I delivered a copy of my book to each new mom's home with an invitation to gather a couple weeks later. I had an online ministry, but right within a block of my home were moms needing encouragement. Suddenly, not moving made the most sense.

A Place of Connection

What if in owning our assigned space we find another layer of humility? We no longer have to parade our opinions, accomplishments, and successes to gain acceptance and approval. We find acceptance and approval by leaning into the people immediately around us. We initiate conversations with our true community instead of shouting into the interwebs, hoping for a thumbs-up from strangers.

In a piece titled "On Humility," Rabbi Jonathan Sacks points out,

> A community is a place of friends. Urban society is a landscape of strangers. Yet there is an irrepressible human urge for recognition. So a culture emerged out of the various ways of "making a statement" to people we do not know, but who, we hope, will somehow notice. Beliefs ceased to be things confessed in prayer and became

slogans emblazoned on t-shirts. A comprehensive repertoire developed of signaling individuality, from personalized number-plates, to in-your-face dressing, to designer labels worn on the outside, not within. You can trace an entire cultural transformation in the shift from renown to fame to celebrity to being famous for being famous.[6]

What if we worried less about whether our words reached the masses and encouraged the one right in front of us? We all wonder, *Do I matter?* We also ask, *Am I loved?* and *Will you be here?* All of these questions come from a place of looking for secure emotional connection.

Last fall, longtime friends of Bruce's parents, the archbishop of Alexandria, Egypt, and his wife, visited Dallas. During our time together, the archbishop told me about *mastabas* in Egypt. A *mastaba* is a bench built into the outside of your home. Lined up side by side they become places of gathering and connection. A space to be reminded, *I am loved, I matter, you are here with me.* Do you have a similar "mastaba" space to gather and connect?

I once had a turquoise picnic table in our front yard. It was an idea inspired by my friend Kristin Schell. The short story is, she fell in love with hosting and cooking while living in France as a high schooler. As an adult she wanted to have people in her home, but her husband was an introvert. So, one weekend she bought a basic picnic table and painted it bright turquoise. She placed it in her front yard and invited some of her neighbors to gather with her there for "Front Yard Fridays."

The week after hearing her story, as I pulled up to our house, I saw that my neighbor across the street had a yard full of picnic tables with a For Sale sign. I called the phone number listed. By that evening I'd met my neighbor Jeff for the first time in the ten years we'd lived there. Not only did he help me cart the table over to my front yard, he offered me his paint gun to make the painting job easier.

I sat at that table with my boys many afternoons, but one stands out in my mind. Our next-door neighbor, Martha, sat down with me while her great-granddaughter ran around the front yard with my youngest son. The little girl's mom had been an eight-year-old girl when we'd moved into our house. Whenever I'd plant flowers, she'd comment on how beautiful they were. Eight years later, as a sophomore in high school, she found herself pregnant around the same time I was pregnant with my youngest. As believers, we can make all the stances about being pro-life, but when a teen chooses life for her baby, how do we show up and support that mom? On that day, it looked like sitting with my neighbor.

Sometimes we believe that in order to live on mission for Christ, we need to go to a foreign country. That sacrificing our comfort is what dying to self looks like. In looking at the boundary line of place, we open our eyes to where God has us physically. What would it look like to lean into the mission field on your block? Have you fully occupied *that* space?

My friend Zubin did this well last summer at family camp when she placed a cooler on her cabin porch. It held chilled drinks, along with a sign inviting counselors to "please take one." A lovely way to do what she could where she was, even if it was only a weeklong stay. Or my friend Mo Aiken, whose family sold their four-bedroom home and most of their belongings. After paying off all their debt, they bought a truck and an RV. They decided to live on mission, traveling across the country, telling others about Jesus. I have another friend who lives in a multimillion-dollar mansion, owns a major NFL team, and shines a light for Jesus in specific rooms with professional athletes and artists most of us will never have access to. Another friend, Una, volunteers her time on the weekends spending the night in a homeless shelter to minister to those who need care and are without a place to stay. All of these are examples of people recognizing where they are, answering God's invitation to join Him, and doing what they can to fill that space.

When we do that, God is free to show off with outcomes we'd never imagine. I had no idea how God would use the relationship with my neighbor Sue that began while taking my boys on a nature walk. I didn't know Sue would have a brain aneurysm that would leave her homebound with hemiplegia. Fast-forward several years to when my mom lived with us and was recovering from chemotherapy. Both women had been instructed by their doctors to exercise. But neither was strong enough to walk the neighborhood alone. So I introduced my mom to Sue, and they began regular walks together.

These two widows became each other's help by humbly filling their assigned spaces. Like Proverbs 15:25 promises, "The LORD tears down the house of the proud but maintains the widow's boundaries" (ESV). In a time when my mom needed a friend and I needed help to support my mom, God provided the perfect person, not because I had made a careful plan or hustled but because I had occupied the space in which He'd placed me in my neighborhood.

Soul Secure

One summer we took a trip to California. On the drive out, we visited the Carlsbad Caverns National Park. After descending 750 feet below the surface level, we explored what Will Rogers is said to have called "The Grand Canyon with a roof over it." After a while of wandering through the cavern, we found a ranger who offered to answer any questions we may have had. My ten-year-old jumped in with, "What would happen to us if a hurricane came here?" The ranger calmly responded, "Oh, hurricanes aren't common in this area of the country."

Then my son moved on to the next weather catastrophe: "What about a tornado?"

"A tornado may damage the building on the surface, but we'd be safe down here."

Personally thankful to hear that response, I then heard my son ask about a more terrifying scenario: "What if there's an earthquake?"

I leaned in to hear his answer to this one. "Well, actually there have been earthquakes in this area. Amazingly, the vibrations go around the cavern, and if you are standing within it, you don't feel the shaking." While my son's questions were motivated by a mix of curiosity and fear, I found it interesting that in these imagined scenarios, inside the cavern was the safest place to be when the earth shook.

My mind filled with all the Scriptures in which David writes about God being his refuge and strength as he is hiding out in caves to escape King Saul. But ultimately, it isn't the hiding that keeps him safe; it's God, who has already decided David will be king. Nothing on earth can harm him and prevent God's promise from being fulfilled.

> If you say, 'The LORD is my refuge,"
>   and you make the Most High your dwelling,
> no harm will overtake you,
>   no disaster will come near your tent.
> For he will command his angels concerning you
>   to guard you in all your ways. (Ps. 91:9–11 NIV)

Not only do we carry the presence of God with us wherever we go, but there is no place we go where we are not surrounded by God. Remember my "God sandwich" analogy? Our soul is surrounded—inside and out—by God's presence. Moses gives Joshua this pep talk before Joshua leads the Israelites into the promised land: "It is the LORD who goes before you. He will be with you; he will not fail you or forsake you. Do not fear or be dismayed" (Deut. 31:8).

Whether we are like Esther, assigned to a palace to advocate for the vulnerable, or like Paul, chained to the wall in a prison while singing praises, God goes before us and with us. We need not fear. Steve Bezner says, "Think about the first two chapters of Matthew. God gives three dreams to Joseph, a poor craftsman, and one dream to the foreign magi. King Herod hears nothing. Which reminds us that your position of power does not dictate God's presence."[7] It's our confession of faith in Jesus that confirms that security.

When I was little, I used to lie completely still in bed with the covers over my head. I was terrified a robber would break into our home through the window above my headboard. (Since I was on the second floor, this wasn't a rational fear.) As an adult that fear was realized. Pulling up to our home after school pickup one day, we saw police cars out front. Someone had smashed through the glass of our back door, gone upstairs to my bedroom, taken a pillowcase, and filled it with my jewelry box. (Sadly for them, it was full of costume jewelry.) They also stole my new laptop.

While I should have felt violated and angry, I was actually filled with incredible gratitude. Thankful we weren't home. Thankful they hadn't stolen the digital camera just two feet from where I'd left my laptop. Thankful I had used Marriott credit card points to buy the computer. Thankful it was a new computer, and the only documents on it were articles I'd written for the God Centered Mom site.

Although I hadn't set up a lock on the computer, I had been working on memorizing Romans 8 and had saved a portion of it as my screen saver. So, turning on my laptop, the thief would be greeted with the words "There is therefore now no condemnation for those who are in Christ Jesus" (Rom. 8:1 ESV).

Although evil, hard circumstances will happen while we occupy our physical place on this earth, nothing can steal our souls. Did I mention that the center of the Carlsbad Cavern is in the shape of a cross? As believers in Jesus's death on the cross and His resurrection, our souls are secure, sealed by the Holy Spirit. Whether we talk about actual physical homes or metaphorical dwellings, we need not fear sin, the vandalism of shalom, because Christ has paid the price of sin. Because of sin's defeat, "I will both lie down and sleep in peace, for you alone, O Lord, make me lie down in safety" (Ps. 4:8). While on this planet, our souls live in a physical body. But once we have confessed belief in Jesus, our souls are eternally secure. There is no fear of death because our eternal life begins at that moment of belief.

DISCUSSION QUESTIONS

1. How do you identify with the country boy with millionaire dreams?

2. Where were you born? In what ways did that place impact your story?

3. How do you feel about where you currently live? Can you relate to a longing for more or different? What would it look like to embrace (even exchange complaints for gratitude about) your current environment?

4. Consider where you spend a majority of your days. What is your divine platform? Who do you frequently come in contact with? How could you intentionally foster a relationship with them?

5. Does fear of bodily harm resonate with you? How does living with your soul secure change your perspective?

Boundary Line of Wiring

May you learn to see your self with the same delight, pride, and expectation with which God sees you in every moment.

John O'Donohue

H is little hand shot up the second the camp counselor asked, "Does anyone know how to beatbox?"

During the talent show, we watched a variety of "skills" on display—from a young gymnast to an impressive pianist (he'd come a long way from when he'd performed eight years before). Each child brought his or her unique gift to share with our camp family. And no matter what happened onstage, each child received a standing ovation and cheers of "We loved it!"

So, when the little boy in front of me raised his hand to perform as a beatboxer, his mom was shocked. But anything is possible at camp. Who was she to hold him back from his beatboxing moment? The little guy bounced up onstage, and then he did something unexpected. As the counselor began to rap a song about pizza, the little boy squatted down and wrapped his arms around his legs. We looked at each other, confused and amused. Then it hit me. He heard the question as, "Does anyone know how to *be a box*?" After watching all the participation from his friends, his heart and hand leapt at the chance to show off his skills. *You want me to be a box? Done.* I wish we would follow that little guy's example and confidently own our unique "boxness." Jump at the chance to activate wiring wherever God places us. I'm guessing most days it's easier for you to see the value in your friends' talents than in your own.

After the "be a box" performance, my oldest son took the stage and sang a fast-paced Christian rap. Since early childhood, he's been comfortable onstage. We have video of him at two years old, standing on a picnic table, executing a passionate rendition of "Take Me Out to the Ball Game." While I'd love to take credit for his confidence and musical ability, it was hardwired into him. We also have three other boys, all with very unique personalities and gifts. One loves to problem-solve and socialize, another prefers a quiet environment to learn about animals or read Harry Potter, and another spends hours creating 3D structures and writing novels. All four boys came from the same set of parents, and all are distinct from each other. All of them were assigned to a similar time in history and place on the planet, but the third boundary line of their God-given spaces is their wiring.

When you look at your God-given space to occupy, what distinguishes you from those around you? It seems that millennials and Gen Zers are better than other generations at taking personality tests and understanding how they uniquely perceive and interact with the world. My husband, Bruce, is a CliftonStrengths coach who helps employees understand their top strengths and places them in job roles that maximize those strengths. He has shown me how, too often, we put more energy into improving our weaknesses or noticing where we fall behind the person next to us than in directing our attention toward our strengths and seeking outlets in which to use them.

While there's freedom in you being you and me being me, the phrase "You can be anything you want to be" actually causes anxiety. Too many choices can lower our level of happiness. It's okay that we are wired to be good at some things and bad at others. In this chapter, I'd love to encourage you to note how God wired you and what talents you have to offer the world. If this personal investigative work feels selfish, don't forget our expanded definition of *humility*: You walk humbly by fully owning your gifts and filling the space you've been given.

Mislabeled Wires

When we were kids, my friend Erika and I would wander through cemeteries, gathering interesting names from tombstones. We'd also write down life-span dates and create imagined stories based on the limited information we found. Some of the names were integrated into our made-up pioneer personas, who wrote letters back and forth as pen pals. When we weren't scoping out tombstones, we were mothering our large number of Cabbage Patch Kids while listening to the local classical station. (Yes, we would call in to make requests.) After reading The Baby-Sitters Club books, we started a club, complete with our own manual and bags. (If my craft retreat didn't make you envious, are you jealous now?)

At Dallas Theological Seminary, one of the professors asks the ministry students to consider what they enjoyed doing as children. The point being that future ministry opportunities are most likely connected to childhood interests. I have to admit, when I look at my childhood interests, they seem to be more odd than anointed. What ministry aligns with hanging out in cemeteries?

But when I examine my childhood a bit more, a theme surfaces: being enthralled with people's stories. I also had a maternal pull. And I loved connecting and communicating with others. When I look at my current space, I see that each of those pieces of my childhood wiring has an outlet, a way to use my interests: sharing others' stories on my podcast, caring for my four boys, and communicating ideas through writing.

How did you spend time when you were a child? Have you ever asked your parents or siblings what you loved? What stories have been told about you as a child? What about the stories and descriptions that are told not with fondness but with annoyance? Maybe you were called bossy or referred to as someone who bounced off the walls. Or you spent hours making messes with paper and markers. Maybe your family, like mine, talks about how you cried for an entire year and were "too sensitive."

Sometimes our natural wiring gets mislabeled as a problem, so we struggle to see the gift in how we were made. Whether a talent is underappreciated by those around us or is an unrefined version that causes repulsion, it's good to dig into our childhood stories to uncover how the gift went sideways.

Personally, my sensitivity felt like more of an inconvenience than a strength. I pleaded with my mom to cut the tags out of my clothes, because they were itchy, and to cut the feet off my footed pajamas, because they made me sweat. Tears flowed easily, and other people often hurt my feelings. Nothing about this aspect of my personhood seemed to be helpful to those around me. It wasn't until I had a supernatural experience with the Holy Spirit, and God revealed Himself through my overly sensitive skin, that I started to see my gift. I noticed how my being comfortable with sadness invited friends to share their hard stories with me. While Buddy from the movie *Elf* may say smiling is his favorite, crying is mine. Can you really have a conversation that matters if tears aren't shed? I kid.

One way the enemy keeps the wiring aspect of our spaces underutilized is by renaming a gift as a problem, something to push aside instead of something to refine. The best way to round out the corners of your giftedness is to meet with the Giver. To ask Him about how He made you and why. John Mayer wrote on Instagram, "Nobody can tell you that you don't have what it takes if they don't fully understand: (a) you (b) what you have (c) what it takes."[1] God understands all three. If He wired you that way, He desires you to use what He gave you for the calling of going and making disciples in your specific God-given space. If you don't know where to begin asking God about your giftedness, don't worry; we'll talk about listening to the Lord in chapter 7.

Another aspect to consider in the boundary line of wiring is your spiritual gifts. In several passages in the New Testament, Paul outlines Holy Spirit–filled gifts available to members of the body of Christ to help spread the gospel. Here is a combined list of the spiritual gifts mentioned in those passages:

1. administration	10. hospitality
2. apostleship	11. knowledge
3. discernment	12. leadership
4. evangelism	13. mercy
5. exhortation	14. prophecy
6. faith	15. serving
7. giving	16. speaking in tongues
8. healing	17. teaching
9. help	18. wisdom[2]

This list seems pretty straightforward but can still cause some confusion. Some Christians believe that not all of these gifts are still given by God. They believe that some of them, like speaking in tongues, were needed for only a specific time in history but not any longer. Fortunately, I don't see anywhere in the Bible that says the Holy Spirit will stop empowering believers to spread the gospel. I don't see any time frame listed for these spiritual gifts.

Growing up, I remember a close family member looking at the list, then looking at me perplexed and saying, "I don't know what your spiritual gifts are." I was a mystery. For decades, I held that statement in my head, feeling like perhaps I was absent the day gifts were passed out. It took me actively engaging in ministry and healing from that memory for God to show me my gifts of faith, exhortation, teaching, and wisdom. Honestly, it's a bit hard to actually type those out, to declare them as true (maybe that's why I buried them in this paragraph). But since they are *spiritual* gifts, I had nothing to do with their creation in me. My only role is to humbly use them in my daily life with others. It is actually prideful to deny those gifts by keeping them hidden and unused.

Beyond your childhood interests and spiritual gifts, another aspect of wiring to consider is what other people come to you for. When someone asks you for help, what do they see you doing well? Often, we discount our wiring as unimportant because it comes easily to us.

A few years ago, not only were life circumstances difficult, but my home was cluttered as well. Thankfully, I knew my friend Kathryn had organizational gifts and a willingness to help. She came over and, in one day, completely transformed my kitchen pantry. My brain struggles to even imagine what an organized space could look like. But that comes easily for Kathryn. So much so that she often doesn't believe us when we shower her with compliments about her gift.

Do you ever do the same thing? Your friends tell you how great you are at speaking or task management or hospitality or prayer, and you push off their admiration? Next time, pay attention to those compliments. They are clues to this boundary line of your space.

Put Me In, Coach

We sat in the parking lot outside the burger place. The whole team, the coach, and the parents were inside celebrating a championship win.

With his lanky legs bent under the hug of his arms, my son cried into his knees. Despite an undefeated season, his heart was crushed. He struggled to be excited about a victory he felt he hadn't helped gain. More a supporter than a participant, he was the only player who watched all of the game from the bench—except the last four seconds. As his coach substituted him in, he explained, "I'm putting you in so you can't say you didn't play."

The message my son received was, "You are the least valuable person on the team." Yes, he held a position on the team, but he hadn't been *in* the game. "I thought I was good at basketball. I worked really hard to practice and get better and I'm obviously not good at all," he said.

I sat next to him in the car, struggling with how to help. Not only did I hate to see my son grieving, but I was supposed to be out of town on a girls' trip. When I'd found out there would be a championship game, I'd delayed my departure. I had sacrificed being with my friends to watch my son play in a game, and instead I watched him sit on a bench.

After joining him in a mini–disappointment party (i.e., empathizing with his sadness), the concept of this book came to me. I attempted to provide perspective. "You know what, buddy? Maybe your job tonight was to cheer on your friends. In order to help secure an important win, you needed to let the five players who were playing well together keep playing. You weren't 'benched'; you were 'placed' for the purpose your coach felt helped earn the victory."

The same is true with the places God assigns us. We can all be on the same team with a secured kingdom victory, but watching from the bench feels less important than playing in the game. We falsely believe that our gifts and talents are contributing less to the win than someone else's. We feel that a person on a conference platform is more vital to the work of making disciples than someone performing administrative work in a cubicle or changing a diaper in the nursery because we don't know how God will use our "bench-warming" moments.

Charaia Callabrass writes,

Sometimes the bench is the place where you are reintroduced to your frail humanity, to your limited capacity, and to His abundant and sufficient grace. Sometimes the bench is where you heal, where you are humbled, and where you are held. Held while you sit letting The Spirit mend you back on your feet. Maybe the bench is the calling away to refine you to what you are called to. Maybe the bench isn't the place you sit to watch life pass you by, but the place you rest and let Christ pass through you.[3]

Will you let Christ pass through you even if it feels like you've been benched?

Historically, the concept of a platform was for the speaker's message to reach everyone in the room, including the people in the back. Being physically lifted higher wasn't a sign of the speaker's significance but a value statement of the listener's position. God desires for His gospel message to reach everyone in your God-given space. Because of how much He values everyone in the world and their relationship with Him, He'll use any means necessary to do it. He isn't interested in numbers. In fact, Jesus often left the multitudes and sought out the one. He wants you to use your gifts right where you are to minister to the ones you are with. If you desire to reach a bigger audience, be faithful to use your gifts where you are and leave the expansion of the boundaries up to Him.

When I was in the season of having lots of little ones in diapers, my college friend Jen called to catch up on our lives. While I cleaned spit-up off my shirt, she traveled around the country as a personal chaplain for a famous Christian music artist. Anytime she wasn't on the road, she spoke at teen conferences. The moment she talked about speaking, a spark lit inside of me, a dream to become a speaker. As soon as the idea surfaced, my reality and doubts squashed it down. What would I even speak about? Who would I speak to? How could I travel and speak while caring for so many little children and a husband who worked a demanding job?

I decided to note my heart's desire and surrender it to God. If it was from Him, He would lead the way in making it a reality at His appointed time. One opportunity He soon brought to my mind was to teach Bible stories to preschoolers on Sunday mornings. With an alphabet-rug "stage," it wasn't a glitzy role. But I have always loved working with kids and using my gift of teaching.

With my heart and mind open to the possibility, God orchestrated a conversation in the preschool hallway with the teacher at the time. I stopped the teacher to ask how he became the storyteller. To my surprise, he was actively looking for a replacement so he could move up with his kids to the early-elementary class. That conversation began four years of me teaching God's Word weekly to three- and four-year-olds.

While it wasn't glamorous, my ability to synthesize the material and make it accessible to my audience was honed. Keeping little ones engaged helped me improve my speaking skills. Teaching through the entire Bible (a few times) improved my Bible literacy. After those four years of teaching the preschoolers, I moved up to teaching kindergarten through second grade. Four years into that gig, I was promoted to teaching third through fifth grade.

Around the same time, my speaking opportunities expanded. Remember in chapter 2 when God invited me to share at our MOPS program? That small step in sharing my testimony launched my mom ministry. After a decade of parenting little ones, I had more than enough challenges and lessons I could offer weary moms. Just a decade after my initial phone call with Jen, not only was I getting paid to speak, but I was traveling around the country to do so. One of those times, I stayed with Jen in Nashville and played with her two little ones. A full 180 in where God had each of us using our talents.

When women share with me a desire to write and teach Bible studies, I encourage them to start where they are with the gifts they have. Invite a small group of women to your home and start teaching those women the Bible. You don't have to wait for a conference-speaking invitation to legitimize your right to fill your current space with your gifts. Trusting God to use your unique gifts in His perfect time and place is a posture of humility.

Christine Caine encourages us along these lines. "I've discovered the reason God does not promote you prematurely is to protect you, not to withhold blessing from you. If the gift of God on you is greater than the character of God within you, it will destroy you. The preparation process is necessary to purify our motives and desires, God has not forgotten you. He's preparing you for the things he's prepared for you. Don't try to bypass the process. Who you're becoming is worth it. The strength you're developing is crucial for the assignment."[4] What we perceive as being benched or as having gifts unworthy of being used is actually God's kindness in refining and developing us for how He wants to use us. Trusting Him in the process of becoming is essential.

We Need You to Be You

Our good friends Amber and Aaron are a lovely example of the phrase "opposites attract." I never laugh harder than when I hear stories of times they've texted on the other's behalf. Once, a female friend visiting from out of town texted Amber and said, "Hey, we'd love to swing by and hang out with y'all. Are you free?" When the text came in, her husband saw it and let Amber know. "Hey, I just saw on your phone Karen texted you and asked if they could swing by and hang out after dinner."

"One hundred percent, yes! I'd love to see them!"

Aaron texted back to Karen, "Sure."

Karen responded, "We don't have to come by if you are busy. Is it really okay if we come over?"

Aaron assured her with, "Yeah."

At the beginning of their visit, Amber wondered what was wrong with Karen. So she asked her, "Is everything okay? Seems like something is going on." Karen explained that she was confused by Amber's texts and that it felt like Amber wasn't interested in having them over. Amber picked up her phone and saw Aaron's dry responses. Nothing even close to how she would have responded. No use of exclamation points. Not even an emoji. While Aaron wasn't deceptively pretending to be Amber, there were ramifications to his acting on her behalf.

Another time, Aaron was driving when Amber saw a text from his friend Brian. "Hey, Aaron, what kind of boots do you have? Where'd you get them from?" Aaron asked her to type, "Ariat. Academy." But she added her own spin: "You're getting new boots!! So fun!" The next time Brian saw Aaron, Brian asked about the text and whether Aaron was making fun of him. When Aaron looked at the phone, he saw Amber's flamboyant response and quickly explained what had happened.

We are all so different. And it's wonderful. But when we get outside of our wiring space and try to be someone else, not only do we confuse people, but we also aren't being who God intended us to be. Pretending to be someone we're not, intentionally or unintentionally, impacts how others perceive and treat us. Sometimes those masks help us blend in with the crowd. Sometimes they give us access to places that we feel provide the significance we desperately desire. Actively accepting your unique giftedness and following God's assignments takes courage.

The other weekend, we watched *Stand by Me* on Friday night and *Good Will Hunting* on Saturday night. Watching them back-to-back, I noticed a theme in the main characters. Both boys are born into lower socioeconomic situations. Their peers expect to have average lives with blue-collar jobs.

In *Stand by Me*, Gordie has a natural gift of writing and telling great stories. Because of his strong friendships, he doesn't want to pursue a different academic path. He is willing to deny his gift to maintain camaraderie. But his friend Chris won't let him. He tells Gordie, "Wish I was your dad. You wouldn't be goin' around talkin' about takin' these stupid shop courses if I was. It's like God gave you something, man, all those stories you can make up. And He said, 'This is what we got for ya, kid. Try not to lose it.' Kids lose everything unless there's someone there to look out for them. And if your parents are too messed up to do it, then maybe I should."[5]

Similarly, in the movie *Good Will Hunting*, the main character, Will Hunting, knows he is a genius but is terrified to leave his predictable life for something better. It's his friend Chuckie who encourages him to move on and use his gifts. Here's a G-rated version of their exchange:

> Chuckie: Look, you're my best friend, so don't take this the wrong way. In twenty years, if you're still livin' here, comin' over to my house to watch the Patriots games, still workin' construction, I'll kill you. That's not a threat; that's a fact. I'll kill you.
>
> Will: Oh, come on! Why is it always I owe it to myself to do this or that? What if I don't want to?
>
> Chuckie: No. No, no, no. No, you don't owe it to yourself. You owe it to me. 'Cause tomorrow I'm gonna wake up and I'll be fifty. And I'll still be doing this stuff. And that's all right, that's fine. I mean, you're sittin' on a winning lottery ticket and you're too scared to cash it in. 'Cause I'd do anything to have what you got. . . . Every day I come by to pick you up. And we go out, we have a few drinks and a few laughs, and it's great. But you know what the best part of my day is? It's for about ten seconds from when I pull up to the curb to when I get to your door. Because I think maybe I'll get up there and I'll knock on the door and you won't be there. No goodbye, no see you later, no nothin'. Just left. I don't know much, but I know that.[6]

Both boys have friends who lovingly let them see how ridiculous it is for them to reject the route to excellence and settle into average. Sometimes stepping into our assigned gifting requires sacrifice of comfort. We have to step out of the pack.

Like David, who bravely volunteers to fight Goliath. David's faith in God and his desire to protect Israel, combined with skills he's gained as a shepherd protecting his flock from wild animals, lead him to stand up to Goliath. King Saul offers his armor to shield David from harm, but the Bible says, "David strapped Saul's sword over the armor, and he tried in vain to walk, for he was not used to them. Then David said to Saul, 'I cannot walk with these, for I am not used to them.' So David removed them" (1 Sam. 17:39).

Pastor Pete Scazzero writes, "David knows himself and he knows the living God who has made the heavens and the earth. With that alone, David is able to break through the barriers of his family's negative views of who he is, the discouragement of Saul, an entire army living in fear, and the curses of Goliath."[7]

King Saul has a complicated relationship with David, to say the least. Although God has chosen Saul to be the first king of Israel (an impressive assignment), when David starts garnering more approval and acceptance from others, Saul feels insecure in his assigned position. That jealousy grows deadly. He becomes obsessed with ending David's life. Saul forgets to fill his space and love God. His eyes drift away from God and away from believing that if God has placed him as king, God is the only one who can replace him.

Poor Saul gets a bad rap, but I can relate to his struggle. I knew God led me to podcasting and that it was an assignment that utilized my gifts of faith, exhortation, teaching, and wisdom. When I attended a conference for Christian podcasters in July 2021, I wanted to quit. It seemed everyone was now doing exactly what I had been doing for years. Comparison strikes again.

Thankfully, first I took my concerns to God, who directed me to this passage in Ecclesiastes: "So I saw that there is nothing better than that all should enjoy their work, for that is their lot; who can bring them to see what will be after them?" (3:22). What stood out to me were the phrases "their work" and "their lot," which focused my attention back on my God-given spaces/work and helped me recognize that I don't know the future ripple effects of doing what has been assigned to me.

Next, I shared my discouragement with my life team. They listened to my feelings and gave me the encouragement I needed, with reminders of all God is doing through my podcast.

Last, a day later, my good friend Kelsey sent me the most amazing text:

> Hey girl! I've NEVER gotten a Jesus dream, but I think I got one for you this weekend! Hold loosely as always and see if this resonates. Many ladies were in what looked and felt like a Whole Foods store. You were going around to different groups in various sections explaining what each of the food items were for. Various grains, various meats, nuts, ice creams, sushi, etc. You were clearly the one who had put the store in place and super knowledgeable about all the produce and products. Women were leaving with bags full of food and excitement.

I had chills reading it. Just like the passage from Ecclesiastes, God was pointing my heart and mind to *serve the people in the store.* Now any time I feel like my efforts are wasted creating podcast episodes, I repeat the phrase, "Serve the people in the store." Women (and some men) come to me looking for help and to connect them with truth and encouragement.

My energy, attention, and gifts are not wasted because other podcasts exist. The harvest is plentiful. Like Aaron Burr humbly acknowledges in his solo in the musical *Hamilton,* "The world was wide enough for Hamilton and Burr." After ending Hamilton's life, Burr realizes their gifts and passions to fight a revolution and establish a nation could have been used in tandem and not in competition. The world had been wide enough for both of them. Similarly, other podcasters' offerings aren't in competition with mine but to be used side by side for kingdom purposes. We are co-laborers for Christ.

You and I are co-laborers. The kingdom comes through you activating your gifts in your assigned time and place. It is worth the time and energy to name your gifts. Think back to your little-girl self and consider how God made you from the start. Reclaim as strengths those parts of you that have been mislabeled as weaknesses. The team needs you even if your position feels less important than the star player's. We definitely like the real you more than you trying to fill someone else's shoes. One more reminder: Owning your gifts and using them in your God-given space isn't prideful but a brave act of humility. I'll be the first one to cheer you on loudly. Go girl!

DISCUSSION QUESTIONS

1. Which personality tests have you taken? How have they helped you understand yourself and others better?

2. What was something you enjoyed doing as a child? Can you see how that activity could inform where and how you minister to others today?

3. Do you relate to my story of having one of your gifts labeled as a problem growing up? What helped you recognize it as a strength instead of a weakness?

4. Have you taken a spiritual gifts quiz? (If not, check out some online, like the one provided by Cru at cru.org.[8]) What gifts did the quiz reveal that you have? Are you using any of them already? Which gift surprised you?

5. How has comparison threatened to derail you from your assigned space? What would "serving the people in the store" look like for you?

Boundary Line of Experiences

Life is never made unbearable by circumstances, but only by lack of meaning and purpose.

Viktor Frankl

The letters hung a bit misaligned on the wall in my assigned craft-retreat bedroom, but they boldly stated, "Act like Coco. Live like Jackie. Dress like Audrey. Laugh like Lucy."

While I'm a huge fan of these female icons and I admit they lived interesting lives, I don't think the goal is for me to emulate each of their journeys, styles, or personalities. As you read in the last chapter, we all benefit when we embrace our unique wiring. The same is true for our life experiences. And yet sometimes in the church we study biblical figures and think we need to follow in their footsteps.

But is that what God desires? For us to replicate the experiences of others, even those from the Bible? My friend Lynn Hoffman once commented to me, "We study everyone else's journey with God, but we don't focus on our own journey." Maybe a better version of that sign could be, "Act like yourself. Live like yourself. Dress like yourself. Laugh like yourself." To take it a step further, I would say to act, live, dress, and laugh like yourself *empowered by God*.

Our experiences serve as stones of remembrance. Not for how great *we* are but for how faithful God is through life's challenges. We retell stories of men and women in the Bible because we want to be reminded of how God used them in spite of their imperfections. In fact, it is often because of their limitations and weaknesses that God gets the glory. That's why the next boundary line for your God-given space is your personal experiences, positive and negative.

Hope Holders

The sound of glass breaking interrupted my routine Monday morning grocery-store run. Minutes later, I left the produce department, rounded the corner into the organic section, and found the source.

Bent over cases of broken IZZE bottles, I saw her with a toddler boy propped on one hip. For a moment, I considered walking past, not wanting to make her feel worse about the situation. But with a Holy Spirit nudge, I asked, "Is someone coming to help you? I can go find help."

This sweet momma paused and said, "They know. I just looked away for a second. I just can't believe it." Her face washed with a mix of shame and embarrassment.

And y'all know I've been there. The spilled Starbucks hot chocolate in the frozen-food department. The son peeing in the middle of a toy store. The tantrum at the checkout over a Lightning McQueen night-light. The public moments that brought me to my knees—both literally, as I cleaned up, and metaphorically, being stripped of my pride. So I comforted her with words of hope. "Oh, it is definitely not what you wanted for your Monday morning. I have four boys and have had my full share of similar moments. Unfortunately, they keep coming. I'm so sorry this happened, but just because it did does not make you a bad mom."

I saw tears start to fill her eyes. Then I warned her, "I'm going to give you a hug." She took it (despite my unshowered, post-workout stench). Because of my past experiences, I was able to come alongside her. You have that to offer someone as well. Your own version of saying yes, it's hard. Yes, you can't imagine life getting better. But the story isn't over. Hope is just around the bend.

Another time, as I entered the cardio room at our gym, I saw a fellow all-boy mom friend. She asked if I wanted to join her, and side by side we climbed automatic stairs while sharing the latest mom challenges. Not only did she encourage me to climb for five more minutes, she also filled me up by pointing out how I have loved my boys well through their challenging behaviors. Her words encouraged me to keep my mom standards high and keep going. I believed her because I knew she understood what my days looked like. Her experience related to my experience. On that day, she brought me the encouragement I needed to do my best and leave the rest to God.

Another friend recently shared about how, while she was going through a divorce, the most encouraging thing she heard was, "This is as hard as it gets." And while she admits that may not have been her hardest day, those words were the ones she needed when she couldn't see what was next.

When you are going through a challenge, isn't that what you want? To know what's coming next? To answer the questions, *Will life ever look the same?* and *How do I keep going?* You just need to know someone who has been where you are and made it through. You need hope. According to *Merriam-Webster*'s dictionary, *hope* is "a desire accompanied by expectation of or belief in fulfillment or success."[1] A desire mixed with belief. To not only want something but also believe in its possibility of happening. Every person's experience differs, but confidence comes in knowing at least one person who survived a similar situation.

Whether it's . . .

- My daily work feels insignificant. But I see how your faithfully showing up for years has led to unexpected opportunities and impact.
- My home is in constant disorder and chaos. But I see your children are grown and your home is tidy.
- My connection to Jesus lacks intimacy. But I see how you have persevered through difficulties, allowed God to heal hurt places, and grown a deep friendship with your Savior.
- My body doesn't function in a way that keeps up with the demands of life. But I see you have found a way to do what needs to be done and forget the rest.

Heading into church one Sunday, I saw a friend leaning on crutches, her left foot in a walking cast. If you had seen her, you may have felt sorry for her (or not). When I saw her standing there, pity wasn't even close to the emotion I felt. Because six months earlier, that friend fought for her life in an out-of-state hospital after a horrific car accident. Fervently we prayed in a crowded church classroom for her physical and emotional healing. Half her body had been crushed and multiple surgeries performed. The full-term baby she'd carried in her womb was now face-to-face with Jesus. So, seeing her standing tall with only a walking boot and crutches? I just about leapt ten feet high. Because despite the loss and grief, our hopes had been realized.

In the midst of trials, the end is blurry and distant. But we can hope. We can seek out someone who has been there and survived. We can move from crushed to walking, even if walking requires a pair of crutches.

A few years ago, I heard Priscilla Shirer preach an incredible sermon. Afterward she had us do an unforgettable prayer activity. She started by saying, "If anyone in this room is struggling in your marriage, whether you are separated, are divorced, or have dealt with infidelity, raise your hand." Around the auditorium hands began to go up. Then she said, "If you have seen God do a miracle in your marriage or have healed from the pain of adultery and/or divorce, then I want you to find a hand and pray over that woman."

We witnessed a powerful moment of God's faithfulness on display. Those in pain being ministered to by those who have walked through to the other side of pain. She continued through various challenges related to family, health, work, and faith. It was a visible reminder that God allows us a chance to minister from our God-given spaces to others in similar places if we follow His invitation.

Running a ministry for women, I have heard a variety of life stories. While we don't compare pasts, there is definitely a range of brokenness and woundedness in every person's life. Growing up, I often felt my kindergarten salvation prayer wasn't a very impressive testimony to convince someone of the gospel's power. Stories of overcoming addiction or abuse seemed to better showcase God's redeeming work. I'll never forget being corrected about that thought process. Someone who had a very hard childhood told me, "I love hearing stories like yours. To know that a child can be spared from woundings is a gift to me. I pray every day for my children to profess salvation at a young age. Your testimony reminds me how my prayer is possible." Embracing our experiences doesn't just include the negative parts of our stories.

If you had parents who loved and obeyed God, then share that truth. If you had a dad who was loving and present, help your friend who is struggling to believe such men exist. If your mom demonstrated selfless care and also followed her God-given gifting, let a mom friend who is wanting to be that kind of mom know. If you have had your needs met and opportunities provided, share that grace so others can expect the same for themselves. Your testimony of provision can be an encouragement.

There are parts of our stories we frequently keep hidden away. Things we struggle to share with friends. Yet I've found that when a friend tells me about her alcoholic father or her former marriage or her child's autism diagnosis, I feel more connected with her. That level of vulnerability and trust only leads to more depth and connection. Dr. Curt Thompson states that "trauma shatters my perspective of my past and of my future. Others help you perceive your story more truly. The enemy would like for you to keep your broken parts hidden—from yourself and definitely from anyone else."[2] What would it look like to bring those experiences into the light so they no longer have the power to hold you back from your current assignment to spread the gospel? What if they actually become the places from which you bring the strongest testimony of God's ability to heal?

My favorite testimony of hope is that our past experiences do not have to define our present or future. I've come to learn that no matter what challenges you've faced in life, God is capable of healing and restoring the broken pieces. The key is to bring your experiences to Him. Allow Him access to the hurt and pain. Then ask Him to reframe the memory so it no longer has a hold on you from the inside out.

Help My Unbelief

While I was researching how experience impacts faith, most of the articles I found argued that our experiences cannot be held in higher regard than our beliefs. The authors feared what would happen if someone acted against the teachings of God's Word because they stood in opposition to their experiences. So the authors determined a choice had to be made between faith and experience. I wonder, does one have to win out over the other? Couldn't we hold them in tandem? I believe we can allow faith and experience to impact each other without disrupting truth. Aligning my beliefs with truth shifts how I experience everyday life. And when my experiences are informed by truth, they affect how I grow in faith.

God made us complex humans with a body, spirit, and soul. Our souls include our thoughts, feelings, and will. I picture the soul settled between the body and the spirit. In Scripture we are commanded, "Keep your heart with all vigilance, for from it flow the springs of life" (Prov. 4:23). The heart is synonymous with the soul. We could rephrase that verse as, "Keep watch over your soul, for from it springs life." Throughout the day, my soul is impacted either by the body (the flesh) or by the spirit (for believers, the indwelling Holy Spirit). In his letter to the Galatians, Paul writes about the pull between the two: "For what the flesh desires is opposed to the Spirit, and what the Spirit desires is opposed to the flesh, for these are opposed to each other, to prevent you from doing what you want" (5:17). We could think of this tension as something that impacts how we experience life.

At IF:Gathering 2022, I heard Dr. Anita Phillips compare our daily experiences and actions to the fruit from a plant. She said clients will come to her wanting to stop a particular behavior pattern. They have tried to remove all the fruit from the tree, but it keeps growing back. Whether that fruit is an addiction, an emotional response, or a pattern of undesirable behavior, making a conscious effort to "just stop" living life that way hasn't changed them. Dr. Phillips said you have to look to the tree which is the source of the fruit. And ultimately you have to look at the soil, which allows for seeds to take root and grow those fruit-producing trees. The soil to be watched over and guarded is your heart/soul.[3] Your daily experiences are directly impacted by the status of your soul. If your soul allows thought patterns to take root, then your behaviors will follow.

One way we can fully occupy our space when it includes experiences is by actively engaging with the status of our souls. When I let my body (instead of the Spirit) influence my soul, my will is swayed to what I deem to be right in the moment. My thoughts then direct my feelings about a situation. But also, as Dr. Lori Desautels writes, "When a continuous stream of negative emotions hijacks our frontal lobes, our brain's architecture changes, leaving us in a heightened stress-response state where fear, anger, anxiety, frustration, and sadness take over our thinking, logical brains."[4] Simply put, our emotions can also hijack our thoughts.

In *The Happiness Hypothesis*, Jonathan Haidt asks us to imagine a rider and an elephant, the elephant being our basic emotional responses and the rider being our logic trying to steer the elephant. He says, "The rider can't just decide to change and order the elephant to go along with the program. Lasting change can come only by retraining the elephant, and that's hard to do."[5] Thankfully, I've found a supernatural option. A way to invite God into past memories to uproot where the emotions started.

Over the past six years, I've prayed with women to heal past memories. Women who've survived childhood abuse and marriage infidelity and tragic loss. Also women who long for deeper intimacy with God and find that something is in the way. With each time of healing (or freedom) prayer, God reclaims what this broken world has stolen. Most of these prayer times start with conversations about a dominant feeling the woman continues to experience— depression, fear, anger, pain. We ask God to reveal a memory of where this emotion started. The goal isn't just to identify the root but to shift the core belief so the soil of her soul does not receive a similar seed of lies in the future.

Because the enemy is crafty and not creative, he preys on the innocent days of youth. When we experience a tragic or even benign circumstance early on, the childhood mind interprets the experience and creates a belief based on what happened.

These don't always have to be overtly traumatic events. For example, after an embarrassing school situation, I might begin to believe, *I have nothing valuable to add*. If my friend has a dismissive alcoholic father, she might begin to believe, *I have to work hard to get the attention and approval of others*.

While the goal is never to retraumatize the one we are praying with, vivid memories come to mind quickly. Sometimes wrong beliefs surface as a form of protection. I may create a vow never to allow an event to happen again. Or I may start to believe something about myself or about God that doesn't line up with the truth. The first step to being set free is to confess the false belief. An example may sound like this: "Lord, forgive me. I've believed that I am responsible for keeping myself and my loved ones safe. I don't believe that You love me enough to protect me from harm. Please forgive me. Help my unbelief." God is incredibly grateful to have our souls align with truth. And like He promises in His Word, He offers abundant grace and forgiveness. His desire is for everyone to walk in the freedom Christ earned on the cross.

After confessing false beliefs, asking for forgiveness, and receiving overflowing grace ("Lord, I accept your love, grace, and forgiveness"), my favorite part happens. We invite Jesus into the memory. No matter whom I've prayed with or what memories we've prayed about, Jesus shows up with the same compassion and love each time. He shifts the atmosphere. One time when I prayed with a friend, she described how the harmful part of her memory faded into black and white while she and Jesus sat together in vibrant color.

These prayer experiences strengthen my faith. They remind me that no experience is beyond God's redemptive reach. Every time we bring a past hurt or wound before Jesus, His compassion reminds us of His loving heart. His desire is for all to be made whole. He wants us to know how Christ's death and resurrection set us free from slavery to sin. And yet I meet so many women paralyzed by sin's effects, standing on the slave platform with their chains cut but not walking in true freedom.

Prophesying that a Messiah would come, Isaiah says,

> The LORD anointed me
> To bring good news to the humble;
> He has sent me to bind up the brokenhearted,
> To proclaim release to captives
> And freedom to prisoners. (61:1 NASB)

The best news comes to the *humble*, those who occupy their God-given spaces, and that message is "You have been set free!" Your

101

story does not define your destiny, but surrendering your story brings God glory.

Several years ago, while I was praying with friends, God revealed to me a soul tie I had with my mom. Maybe that term is unfamiliar to you like it was to me. My friends told me a soul tie is any person whose approval, attention, and value statements are stronger in my heart and mind than God's. Someone who occupies more of my mental energy than God does. It could be a parent, spouse, child, past boyfriend—anyone whose words echo in my mind or whose reaction I obsess over or approval I fear losing.

When we were praying through one of my memories, the other two gals picked up on a soul tie with my mom. They began to ask questions, and we asked for God to reveal a physical object connecting me and my mom. I've prayed with women whose soul ties were objects like a rope or a hose or an arrow. In my case, I saw a twenty-foot-thick wooden beam between my mom and me.

While I had never considered how we could be attached but still emotionally distant, that image made complete sense. Unlike a rope or a hose, a wooden beam doesn't bend. No matter how much my mom and I desired to be close or what efforts we put toward our relationship, the distance remained. Then my friends asked me how we were attached to the beam. That's when I realized it was coming out of my mom's chest. Although it was an odd picture, it confirmed to me how my mom did not desire for that beam to separate us. It was projecting from her own place of brokenness and pain. When the girls instructed me to mentally saw the beam in half and break the soul tie, for the first time in my life, I felt overwhelming compassion for my mom's story. I wanted to help heal all the pain and heartache of her past. The girls then prompted me to hand my mom over to Jesus. To be released from the burden of her healing journey.

Not only did I experience a closer connection with God because of that experience, but also this time of prayer happened just months before my mom came to live with me for a year. With the soul tie broken, I realized I had wasted unnecessary energy fighting past lies and critical inner monologues in daily interactions with my mom. Also, after I surrendered my mom's spiritual healing journey to Jesus, she walked through her own health crisis, the loss of my dad, and an uprooting from her community in Costa Rica. A reminder that God was working in my mom's heart, mind, and soul, and His work wasn't dependent on me.

One aspect of embracing experiences as part of my God-given space was trusting that God would provide in ways I couldn't have known to prepare for. After we prayed through breaking off the soul tie with my mom, God also set me free from spirits of weakness, fear, and lies. That freedom came before I walked through the hardest challenge of my life to this point—dealing with the loss of my dad and the care of my mom. Where I may have succumbed to lies, weakness, and fear, instead I faced the trials with truth, strength, and faith. I learned to trust in God for the daily grace to walk through impossible days.

Pain Not Wasted

Pain is part of life. But if we fully occupy the space of our experiences, our pain is not wasted but serves as a platform to go and make disciples. This reminds me of the apostle Paul. The first mention of Paul is actually with his given name, Saul, at the stoning of faith-filled Stephen. We read, "Then they dragged him out of the city and began to stone him, and the witnesses laid their coats at the feet of a young man named Saul" (Acts 7:58). The very next chapter begins, "And Saul approved of their killing him" (8:1).

Saul leads the persecution against the church by imprisoning men and women who confess belief in Jesus and are followers of the Way. His experience up to this point is as a Roman citizen and devout Jew. Both parts of his story explain a bit of why he adamantly opposes those who claim the Messiah has come. Saul does not believe Jesus is God, and Jesus claiming to be God when

Saul believes He is not is blasphemy in Saul's mind. He feels it is his duty as a follower of God to punish those who claim Jesus as the Savior. As a devout keeper of the Law, Saul is obeying the command in Leviticus 24:16, "One who blasphemes the name of the LORD shall be put to death; the whole congregation shall stone the blasphemer."

Thankfully, his past experiences and unbelief are not the end of the story. On Saul's way to the city of Damascus to arrest more followers of the Way, Jesus changes the narrative. "Suddenly a light from heaven flashed around him. He fell to the ground and heard a voice saying to him, 'Saul, Saul, why do you persecute me?' He asked, 'Who are you, Lord?' The reply came, 'I am Jesus, whom you are persecuting. But get up and enter the city, and you will be told what you are to do'" (Acts 9:3–6). Physically blinded by the experience, Saul is led by others into the town.

Meanwhile, Ananias, a disciple in Damascus, receives a spiritual vision from God asking him to go to Saul and heal his sight. Rightfully so, Ananias questions this assignment, given Saul's reputation and authority to imprison him. God gives Ananias a glimpse into how He will reframe Saul's experience for the spread of the gospel. "Go, for he is an instrument whom I have chosen to bring my name before gentiles and kings and before the people of Israel" (v. 15). Ananias bravely goes to Saul and heals him. After some days with the disciples in Damascus, "immediately [Saul] began to proclaim Jesus in the synagogues, saying, 'He is the Son of God'" (v. 20).

Saul correctly aligns his beliefs with the truth and does not allow his past to disrupt his future ministry. In fact, it is because of his past as a Roman citizen and devout Jew that Saul gains access to exclusive audiences. When Saul launches his ministry to the gentiles in Acts 13, we see Luke begin to use the Greek title "Paul" instead of the Hebrew "Saul."

In Philippians 3:5–6, Paul acknowledges all he'd had going for him: "circumcised on the eighth day, a member of the people of Israel, of the tribe of Benjamin, a Hebrew born of Hebrews; as to the law, a Pharisee; as to zeal, a persecutor of the church; as to righteousness under the law, blameless." Because of his heritage, Paul is invited to speak to groups of the Jewish community and the Roman leaders. Paul understands that God assigned him, before birth, for the purposes He has set aside for him to do. And his experience, his testimony, causes others to believe in the good news of Jesus.

In his letter to the Galatians, Paul says, "They only heard it said, 'The one who formerly was persecuting us is now proclaiming the faith he once tried to destroy.' And they glorified God because of me" (Gal. 1:23–24). If our expanded definition of *humility* is to fully occupy our God-given spaces, then Paul humbly occupies the space of being the former persecutor who now proclaims the gospel.

A key part of being a disciple of Jesus who makes other disciples is crafting your testimony, the culmination of faith experiences communicating the power of the gospel in your life.

I have never been an addict. I haven't experienced the pain of divorce. I haven't walked through seasons of infertility. There are spaces I am not meant to occupy and minister, but maybe you are. Women exist who are longing to hear your story of transformation. You hold the hope they are struggling to grasp. The only thing standing in the way is acknowledging the boundary line of experience, fully embracing your story instead of rejecting it.

The one topic I bring up the most in conversations is God's ability to heal us and free us through prayer. Like Paul repeating his testimony to whomever would listen wherever God placed him, I will testify to the Spirit's work in my life to set me free. I will take a moment in the space of this book to plead on behalf of your life. Do not let your past experiences hold you back from the good purposes God has planned for you. If you desire deeper intimacy with Jesus, find a freedom-prayer ministry in your city or via Zoom, or start one, and be set free. This same Jesus is available to all of us through the indwelling of the Holy Spirit. Your redeemed story has the power to remind others of the truth of the Good News. Even beyond what your story can do for others, I can't wait to meet you and hear how you are freely walking with Jesus in the space He's given you to occupy.

DISCUSSION QUESTIONS

1. How have you experienced someone extending hope to you in a hard season?

2. What parts of your past uniquely position you to be a holder of hope for someone else?

3. What past experiences do you feel need to be healed by God?

4. If you are willing, share with a trusted friend and perhaps consider gathering for a time to pray through healing that memory.

5. When it comes to going and making disciples, how has your past experience, like Paul's, allowed you access to certain groups of people and a testimony that displays the gospel's power?

Draw Up Your Space
WORKSHEET

Now, let's piece those boundary lines together and determine your current God-given space. You may have already answered some of the following questions at the end of each chapter, but I wanted to provide a way for you to bring all that information together in one place.

You may choose to answer the questions below directly on these pages. Or you could choose to use a separate journal to answer them. Personally, I'm a journal girl. Not only do I appreciate having a record of past processing, but I've also found drawing up my God-given space is not a once-and-done exercise. Whenever I feel stuck, insecure, confused, or in need of direction, working through these questions helps give me the comfort and clarity I need. Because over time, spaces shrink, swell, or shift. Answering these questions should help you understand the goodness of where you are and your next right step.

1. Boundary of Time:

Consider your story from the largest measure of time (your historical timeline) down to your minute-to-minute experience (your present moment). Evaluate how the concept of time plays into your current space.

• What details stand out in your birth story? What had to come together to bring you into this world?

_____

_____

_____

• What is significant about what is happening right now in history related to your story (e.g., culture, technology, current events, etc.)?

_____

_____

_____

• Describe your current season in regard to the hard (pruning) and the good (fruitful):

_____

_____

_____

* What's unique about this next stretch of time for you (the next month, year, season)? What sets it apart? Does it impact or change your perspective on your space (e.g., new job, child starting school, or ill parent needing your help)?

_____

_____

_____

* What occupies your day-to-day moments? What do you spend the majority of your time doing? Do you have a choice in how you spend your time?

_____

_____

_____

2. Boundary of Place:

In this section, consider the physical aspects of your God-given space. Start broadly from the global level and narrow down to the space between your two feet.

* In what part of the world were you born?

_____

_____

_____

- Describe the positives and negatives of where you currently live (your neighborhood):

- What places do you frequently visit (e.g., locations for work, leisure, education, errands)?

- Thinking about your personal physical space (which includes your body), what occupies a majority of your thoughts, time, and energy? How might you impact the world around you (consider your hands, your heart, your mind, your words)?

3. Boundary of Wiring:

There is only one you. A key aspect of your unique space is how you are made. Even if some of your gifts have been mislabeled as weaknesses, pulling all these answers together should help you embrace your special God-given wiring.

• What did you spend time doing as a child?

_____

_____

_____

• What are some negative labels you received as a child that you can now see were actually mislabeled strengths?

_____

_____

_____

• If you have taken a personality test before (like Myers-Briggs, CliftonStrengths, or the Enneagram), write down all the personality info you received:

_____

_____

_____

_____

• Take a spiritual gifts quiz and write the results here:

_____

_____

_____

_____

_____

• What do people come to you for advice or help with?

_____

_____

_____

4. Boundary of Experiences:

Our lives are a mix of positive and negative experiences. Acknowledging the gifts of both helps define whom we can receive help from and whom we can extend hope to.

• What challenge are you currently experiencing for which you need hope FROM someone else?

_____

_____

_____

• What part of your story uniquely positions you to give hope TO someone else?

_____

_____

_____

• What past trial/wound/challenge have you kept to yourself that needs healing?

_____

_____

_____

• What moment(s) in your life can be a testimony of healing or redemption to reveal God's goodness to others?

_____

_____

_____

My hope is that as you work through this exercise, God will enlighten your heart to define the space He's given you. If you're still unsure what to do next, keep reading! In the next chapter, you will learn about having a discerning heart so you can listen to God's voice. After reading that chapter, come back to these questions and ask God to direct your answers.

FULLY OCCUPYING YOUR GOD-GIVEN SPACE

After drawing up your God-given space, your next step is to evaluate if you are filling that space. Part of filling the space will require analyzing if you are shrinking back from an obvious invitation God is extending or if you are spending a lot more energy in other people's spaces to avoid what God has for you. Sometimes we know where God is placing us but don't have the confidence to own it. Another aspect of making sure we fully occupy our space includes doing some tending work to clear out the things that distract and deter us. I want to encourage you to embrace your space even if it looks nothing like you'd imagined.

God-Listening Heart

God speaks in the silence of the heart. Listening is the beginning of prayer.

Mother Teresa

Drying off from my shower, I heard the doorbell ring. My youngest son yelled up to me, "Mom! It's your friend. Come downstairs!" I threw on clothes and wondered who could be visiting me on a Saturday morning. As I headed down the stairs, my son said, "I thought it was your friend, but it's a lady and a boy."

After reminding him of the importance of not opening the door to strangers, I asked, "Are they still here?" He nodded, and I opened the door to find a cute mom in a ball cap and a "#momlife" tee.

She quickly introduced herself. "I'm your neighbor the next street over. I remember a few years ago you had a sign in your front yard asking if people needed prayer. We are in a hard place right now." Her eyes filled with tears. "I thought you could help."

Amazed at her bravery (and memory), I invited her in as my hair dripped. My plan had been to get ready, take the boys to get haircuts, then head to the local IF:Gathering. Instead, we sat in my living room and I listened to this mom pour out her deep desire for community. Her family attended a church, but it was farther out in the suburbs, and most of their community life happened too far from our neighborhood. She shared how their family had considered moving last year, but God made it clear that He wanted them to stay, and He showed her that even though moving would make community convenient, it wasn't what He had for them. When they'd decided not to move, she'd thought she would find her people through a new homeschool cooperative her friend was starting in the fall. But she'd just learned that her friend had decided to put her children in public school and no longer start the group. With that news, her dream of finally having people to do life alongside had been shattered.

She came to my door looking for wisdom and guidance, curious to learn about my church and about opportunities for deep, meaningful community. I shared what I knew about various churches in our area that may fill her need. Then I told her about the moms living on our block whom I'd met in the last year. We began to brainstorm gathering these moms together, both of us occupying the spaces in which God had placed us.

Before she and her son left, I asked her if she'd like a copy of my book *Don't Mom Alone*. She enthusiastically responded, "You wrote a book? I had no idea! I absolutely want a copy." Once again God confirmed His timing in my obedience. Technically, I was supposed to write the book you're reading first. It's the one I pitched to publishers in 2019. And the one my publisher expected me to write. But when I had been looking for a publisher, several other ones had asked, "Why aren't you writing a Don't Mom Alone book to go along with your current ministry?" Honestly, my answer was a bit pathetic. Writing a book to moms with the same title as my podcast felt too obvious, not very interesting, and definitely not creative. Their question did cause me to pause. And I decided to ask God what He thought.

He directed me to consider the boundary lines of my space. Starting with the time boundary line: I was actively mothering but no longer in the thick of the early years. I was close enough to remember the challenges but not so overwhelmed by them that I didn't have hope to offer. As far as place, I had just been offered a two-book contract, which allowed me the opportunity to write a book for moms first. My divine platform included thousands of moms around the world who tuned in to the podcast weekly. Regarding the wiring and experience boundary lines, like I shared before, I love connecting and communicating. Being able to connect a lonely, overwhelmed mom with encouragement and resources she would need fired me up. That I had spent the last ten years writing and recording based on my own isolated mom experience felt like a key boundary line.

Then God asked me to consider whether I had filled the space we had just outlined. Even though I had produced over three hundred podcast episodes, published years of blog posts, and shared regularly on social media, I didn't have a smaller, consumable option to hand a mom. If I met a desperate mom (like the one who ended up knocking on my door), it would be a bit overwhelming to say, "Go listen to these three hundred hours of content." But with a book, I could share all the things I wished I could tell her over several cups of coffee. It would multiply God's current assignment for me.

So, with no outline or idea of what would be included in the book, I started writing *Don't Mom Alone*. By following God's lead, we released a book on fighting against isolation in the midst of a pandemic. A detail God was fully aware of but obviously none of us expected. I also had a book I could give a neighbor who knocked on my door, looking for help on a hard day.

Good or Godly

Even when we draw up our God-given spaces on paper, sometimes we still wonder, *Is this just my idea or God's?* There are plenty of really good spaces we can occupy, but how do you and I discern which one is for us? In the face of big or small decisions, having too many choices can lead to not taking any action. Or sometimes a choice makes logical sense, and we move forward without checking in with God to see if it's where He's leading us. For instance, King David had a good idea to build a temple for God, but was it God's idea?

After David dances in the streets celebrating the return of the ark of the covenant (remember, this was where God's presence dwelt), he calls in his prophet Nathan and says, "I dwell in a house of cedar, but the ark of God dwells in a tent" (2 Sam. 7:2 ESV). Nathan responds with, "Go, do all that is in your heart, for the LORD is with you" (v. 3 ESV). Basically, Nathan agrees this is a good idea. Yes, go do that thing your heart has led you to do. But then God speaks to Nathan (remember, a prophet hears from God and declares what they hear to others).

> Go and tell my servant David, "Thus says the LORD: Would you build me a house to dwell in? I have not lived in a house since the day I brought up the people of Israel from Egypt to this day, but I have been moving about in a tent for my dwelling. In all places where I have moved . . . did I speak a word . . . saying, 'Why have you not built me a house of cedar?'" (vv. 5–7 ESV)

God continues by reminding David of the space He's given him. How He has taken David from the pasture and made him a king. How He has been with David wherever he's gone and cut off his enemies. How He will make a great name for David, one of the greatest on earth.

> And I will appoint a place for my people Israel and will plant them, so that they may dwell in their own place and be disturbed no more. . . . I will give you rest from all your enemies. Moreover, the LORD declares to you that the LORD will make you a house. . . . I will raise up your offspring . . . and I will establish his kingdom. He shall build a house for my name. (vv. 10–13 ESV)

God sets David straight. He's never asked him to build a temple. In fact, it is God who has built an "eternal kingdom" for David. Also, God assigns David's son Solomon to build a permanent temple for God's presence to dwell.

God appoints the spaces, and He assigns the work we are to do. Even if what we come up with seems like a good idea, it may not be God's timing or purpose for us.

In order to tell the difference between what is logical and what is led by God, first present the idea to God. Then learn how to listen for His guidance. Personally, while I may have grown up knowing I *should* ask God about decisions, no one taught me how to discern His voice to gain His wisdom.

My husband's life verse is James 1:5: "If any of you is lacking in wisdom, ask God, who gives to all generously and ungrudgingly, and it will be given you." Our world is full of information, but so often we lack wisdom, particularly when there is a decision to be made. The fear of making the wrong choice can paralyze us from making any choice. That's why I love that James clarifies in the next verse, "but ask in faith, never doubting" (v. 6). When looking for wisdom, we should come to God with a posture of faith, not fear.

King Solomon watched as his father, David, sought God faithfully (even with a few missteps), and he witnessed God's steadfast love toward David in return. When it was Solomon's turn to lead Israel, he understood the magnitude of the role. Perhaps that's why, when God appears to Solomon in a dream and asks what he wants, Solomon responds, "But I am only a little child and do not know how to carry out my duties. . . . So give your servant a discerning heart to govern your people and to distinguish between right and wrong. For who is able to govern this great people of yours?" (1 Kings 3:7, 9 NIV).

When Sunday school teachers share the story of Solomon, they talk about him asking for wisdom. Here we see that he asks for a "discerning heart."

The Hebrew words for "discerning heart" are *shema lev*. *Lev* is often translated "heart" or "soul."[1] The word *shema*[2] is the same word used in 1 Samuel 3:9 when Eli instructs a young Samuel in how to respond to God's call. "Speak, Lord, for your servant is listening" could be translated, "Speak, Lord, for your servant *shema*." It's also the first word in the Hebrew prayer of the same name, the Shema, which begins "Hear, O Israel: The Lord is our God, the Lord alone" (Deut. 6:4).

Solomon's father, David, was a man after God's own heart. Solomon asked for a heart that listened to God. In the last chapter, I mentioned how our souls can be pulled toward the Spirit or toward the world. Solomon was asking for a soul that pulled toward a spiritual direction, not a logical one.

Know His Voice

What I found interesting while researching the concept of *shema* is how listening is tied to obedience. In the Hebrew culture, you wouldn't just hear from the Lord; you would act on what you heard. One would never separate hearing from obeying. So when Solomon asked for wisdom, he desired a God-listening heart in order to hear from God and to obey His commands.

In my first job as a speech-language pathologist, I worked with children who either were born deaf or had become deaf in infancy. The clinic where I worked received a grant to provide free cochlear implantation for low-income families. Frequently, the parents who sought cochlear implants were not a part of the amazing deaf community. They desired to connect with their children in a hearing world. Not only was this life-transforming surgery costly, but it required significant healing time before the device could be activated.

One of the most rewarding days at this job was the day of activation. In a quiet room, the audiologist would sit by the equipment to allow a gentle introduction of sound for the child. Meanwhile the parents would sit across from their precious little one and wait for the audiologist to give them the signal that it was okay to start speaking. Hearing sound for the first time can be a bit terrifying, and the goal was not to cause more trauma.

What amazed me was the similarity in experiences every time we activated the device. One of the parents would softly repeat the child's name: "Hi, Molly! Molly . . ." Then they would say the words they'd longed for their child to hear since birth: "We love you. Mommy and Daddy love you." Identity and worth. These parents long for their daughter to hear her identity ("Molly") and worth ("We love you").

If you need a good cry, I highly recommend googling cochlear implant activation videos. Because what strikes a chord in our own hearts is a longing to hear the same thing from our heavenly Father. To know who we are and what He thinks about us. Through God's Word and the indwelling of the Holy Spirit, we have access to knowing our true identity and worth. So often in trying to decide between two options or gain wisdom on a decision, clarity could come from trusting the identity and worth God places on us instead of seeking them in the approval and acceptance of others.

While Molly's parents felt comfort knowing they could finally tell their daughter who she was and how they felt about her, unfortunately, it would take lots and lots of time and therapy for her brain to interpret the sounds she heard. A big part of my job was to train clients to differentiate one sound from another. We would start with basic differentiation, like hearing the difference between a knock on the door and a voice saying their name. Then we would move into finer speech discrimination.

It was tedious, repetitive work, but the goal was to refine and train their ability to listen. The more clearly they differentiated sounds, the better their ability was to speak. My supervisor used to say, "You talk the way you hear." It was often her way of knowing if the batteries in a child's device had died. After a $10,000 surgery, recovery, and hours of therapy, if the implants' few-dollar batteries were dead, a child couldn't hear. And without hearing, he or she struggled to clearly communicate.

Even though Solomon asked for a God-listening heart, at some point he stopped seeking God's direction. He leaned on his own logic over listening. Like Solomon, or as with a battery-less implant, we can have God's Spirit in us and an ability to hear from Him but not actively tune in to His instructions for us. Even if we desire to listen, as with the cochlear implant patients, it takes time to train sound discrimination and attribute meaning to sounds. Listening to God's voice takes familiarity and intimacy. Like sheep knowing their shepherd's voice.

Another thing you should google is "Do sheep follow the voice of their shepherd?" then watch some of the videos that come up. You'll watch as several people try to call the sheep, but it's when the shepherd calls that the sheep stop what they are doing and respond. When Jesus uses the example of sheep, He knows His audience is very familiar with the concept. "The sheep hear his voice. He calls his own sheep by name and leads them out. When he has brought out all his own, he goes ahead of them, and the sheep follow him because they know his voice. They will not follow a stranger, but they will run from him because they do not know the voice of strangers" (John 10:3–5).

Sometimes we think we know a better space we should occupy than the one God is assigning us. The grass looks greener on the other side, and so we wander off from God's direction. As counselor and teacher John Eldredge says, we would do better to "stay close. Listen for his voice. Let him lead."[3] One way we can become familiar with God's voice is by making it a habit to read His Word. When we've spent an abundant amount of time reading the Bible, we can more easily discern whether thoughts that come into our minds sound like promptings from the Holy Spirit.

Often, I think those who struggle with the concept of hearing from God have experienced misuse of the phrase "God told me." Warning bells go off for me when that phrase introduces an idea or concept that runs counter to how God has operated for centuries or in direct opposition to the structure He's given us for good lives. But it's a different situation if what you've heard from God runs counter to the logical solution your friend is offering you. God doesn't follow human logic. He consistently flips the script on power structures. "But God chose what is foolish in the world to shame the wise; God chose what is weak in the world to shame the strong" (1 Cor. 1:27). Thankfully, He doesn't leave us wondering or wandering but offers to lead us. But that requires learning to engage in the "dynamic dialogue with the Lover of our souls," as authors Mark and Patti Virkler put it.[4]

"Prayer is not making speeches to God; it is entering into conversational intimacy with him," Eldredge says.[5] After reading God's Word, we can allow space to quiet our hearts and minds, listen to Him, and pray an invitation similar to Samuel's: "Speak, Lord, for your servant is listening." We can even ask God, like the disciples did, "Lord, teach us to pray" (Luke 11:1). Try the four keys the Virklers offer for learning to hear God's voice:

1. Stillness: Quiet yourself so you can hear God's voice.
2. Vision: Look for vision as you pray.
3. Spontaneity: Recognize God's voice as spontaneous thoughts that light upon your mind.
4. Journaling: Write down the flow of thoughts and pictures.[6]

These steps remind me of the prophet Habakkuk, who "keep[s] watch to see" (2:1) and waits for an answer from God. He says, "Then the Lord answered me and said: Write the vision; make it plain on tablets" (2:2).

Are we expectant that God will answer? As I mentioned in the last section, in reference to James 1:6, do we seek wisdom from God in faith or from a place of fear? Do we trust that if we wait, God will answer, even if it takes time or the answer isn't the one we want to hear? In Habakkuk's action to "keep watch to see," the Hebrew word for "watch" is *tsaphah*, which means "to lean forward, to peer into the distance, to observe, to wait for."[7] If, like Habakkuk, we lean forward, wait, and tune our God-listening hearts to Jesus, not only will He enlighten the eyes of our hearts (see Eph. 1:18), but the things of this world will grow strangely dim. The path to the next space God has for us to occupy will become clearer.

Is That for Me?

Paul writes to the Romans, "Do not be conformed to this age, but be transformed by the renewing of the mind, so that you may discern what is the will of God—what is good and acceptable and perfect" (12:2). I want to narrow in on the phrase, "so that you may discern." Discernment is valuable in knowing right where I belong. In my times of prayer and listening, I can ask God to help me discern His good will because being out of line with God's will could lead to more harm than good.

I have one son who was wired to be a helper. At three years old, he'd pick up my dropped keys without being asked. He's the one with whom I have had many conversations about how and when to help others. We also talk about how sometimes trying to save someone can actually cause bigger problems. Like if someone is drowning, your job is to alert the lifeguard. If you try to be the rescuer, you both could end up drowning. As a teenager navigating the Wild West of the internet, he's had to learn the hard way to pause before jumping in to help.

A few months ago, this son opened a direct message on Instagram from a friend pleading with him to help her out. She wrote, "My old phone just went bad, and I am trying to link my page to my new device, and they asked me to find someone to help me receive a help code, just to verify if I am the right person trying to link to the account. Will you help me with it please?" Then she sent one more message: "It is important please [praying hands emoji to solidify her need]." You'd think, *What could be the harm in helping a friend recover her account?* The problem was that the message came from a hacker posing as his friend. Helping in this case led to hacking. Clicking that link allowed the evil internet troll to get access to my son's account and change his password and recovery contact information. Then the hacker went on pretending to be my son and tried to bamboozle my son's friends via DM. Thankfully, some friends and family members texted us to ask if it was really him. They went one step further to figure out, *Is it my job to help or not?*

So often, I think we feel pressure to help all the people and all the causes. That's just too much weight to bear. It's assuming that the rescue of the world is up to you. Here's the good news: There is one Savior, and you're not Him.

In the 2002 version of *Spider-Man*, Peter Parker's uncle Ben gives him the advice, "With great power comes great responsibility."[8] He wants Peter to know that as Spider-Man, he has the ability to use his powers for good or to cause harm. If he wants to get revenge on a bully, he can. If he wants to stir up trouble just for kicks, he is able to. But choosing when and where to use his powers takes discernment and responsibility.

In the newest *Spider-Man* movie, *No Way Home*, Peter's aunt May shares the same quote: "With great power comes great responsibility."[9] Unfortunately, her intention is very different from the original. She is trying to convince Peter that it is his responsibility to rehabilitate the villains who have been brought into Peter's dimension. Her hope is that by becoming "good guys," they will evade being killed in their own dimensions. Instead of hearing a message to use his powers for good, he is burdened with using his powers to make others good. To fix them and save them. While I agree there is Scripture to support our doing good and helping care for the needs of others, it is never our responsibility to make someone good, fix brokenness, or save anyone. If that were true, we would take the place of God in His redeeming work in the world.

It seems that Gen Z is more aware than ever of the brokenness of this world. With globalization and social media, a natural disaster or traumatic event pops right in front of us the moment it happens. As moral beings, it makes sense that we want to help when we see someone in trouble. Unfortunately, I think we become so burdened by all the trouble of the world that we don't feel like we can do anything to help. But by doing nothing, we feel guilty. Then we pile on shame, believing something is wrong with us because we are not helping fix X, Y, and Z.

Does that mean you and I are off the hook? Nope. Unfortunately, I think we can swing the other way, shrugging off all responsibility to care for the needs of those around us. If we bury our heads in our Bibles and ignore the pain of the world, we are of no earthly good. If we put all our energy and attention into solving social issues without any grounding in the truth of the gospel, we don't offer eternal hope. If we spend all our time worshiping and praying and filling our souls with the presence of God but don't engage the world empowered by the Spirit, then we are just a charismatic show tickling our own sensory systems. There is a balance at play between word, power, and deed.

This is where I want to bring freedom with the message of *Right Where You Belong*. My hope is to help you feel like filling the space where you are with your unique wiring and experiences is enough. Not only is it enough, it's all God has asked of you: to humbly make kingdom impact by fully occupying your God-given space. Like my friend Candace Cartwright, a stay-at-home mom turned not-for-profit president, did.

One boundary line of Candace's God-given space included her past trauma. She was familiar with fleeing in the middle of the night from an abusive father. Her mother's dysfunctional family history made Candace curious why no one rescued her mom as a child. Listening to the Lord one night led Candace to discern her assignment and occupy her current space.

"I was rocking my 3-week-old son and I had this moment where I just knew we were supposed to adopt," Cartwright says. "It was so clear—as if God were saying, 'This is what I have for you.'"

She told [her husband] about it but let him know she was not ready to talk about it for a long time.

"Not for a year," she laughs. "That was our deal."

A year later, Cartwright and her husband attended their first foster care interest meeting.[10]

When their first fostering placement arrived at their house with his belongings in a trash bag, Candace had another idea. This time she rallied friends through a Facebook page to put together a project called My Very Own Bag. Bringing their skills and resources together, her community provided bags for children in the foster care system. Since her first prompting from God, Candace has been a Court Appointed Special Advocates (CASA) volunteer, she has fostered and adopted her son, Owen, and she has become acquainted with her county's child welfare system.

At each impasse, she's followed God's lead. My favorite part of her story is how God directed her and her husband to start Foster Love Bell County, a nonprofit created to support their local child-welfare system. In 2018, thanks to generous donors and a partnership with three local businessmen, they were able to purchase a home to be used by their local case workers.

> Little by little, the needs began to grow. . . . We would hear that conference space was hard to come by, so we would put that on the list. And then we knew kids sometimes had to wait in offices for long periods of time, so we thought, "Oh, we can make a space for them to come and play and hang out," instead of being in an office setting. Everything just kind of grew and grew into what you see today. We thought this property would be perfect to meet all of those needs.[11]

Now this historic home is a beacon of hope for children moving from broken homes into foster care. So, while we may be overwhelmed by the global problem of dysfunctional families and orphans, Candace models listening for God's unique prompting in your spirit and using your gifts and interests right where you are.

Solving all the problems of the world is not our full responsibility. But if we each do what we can where we are, as God leads, we make an impact. Consider the boundary lines you've drawn up for your space, and bring them to God in listening prayer. If you've never brought a decision to God and listened for His response, then that is your next step. Like my cochlear implant clients, tune your God-listening heart to your Shepherd's voice. Lean forward with expectancy and allow Him to give you discernment and direction on filling your God-given space.

DISCUSSION QUESTIONS

1. How would you have responded if a stranger rang your doorbell and asked for help?

2. What are some of the decisions you've had to make recently? Did you struggle to discern whether they were just good ideas or God's ideas? What helped you make your decision?

3. Have you been taught how to listen to the Lord? If you've never tried to sit in silence and listen, what has kept you from trying it out?

4. Do you struggle with feeling an overwhelming responsibility for all the brokenness in the world? What are your thoughts on the phrase "With great power comes great responsibility"?

5. How are you currently using your gifts and past experiences to help others around you?

EIGHT

Shrink or Swell

Every Christian has the choice between being humble and being humbled.

It is not humility to underrate yourself. Humility is to think of yourself as God thinks of you. It is to feel that if we have talents God has given them to us.

Charles Spurgeon

After we showed the usher the orchestra-section tickets we'd purchased last minute, he led my son and me to our seats. When we settled in for our first Broadway show, the warmth of excitement mixed with several layers of clothing quickly hit us. In the awkward attempt to pull our arms out of our coats without knocking out fellow patrons, we started a conversation with a cute couple next to us. We were already deep into swapping stories about how the pandemic had impacted the last few years when the usher returned to let us know we were in the wrong seats. Same row; we just needed to move to the other side of the aisle. Apparently we were occupying someone else's space.

The thing about theater seats is you can fill only one at a time. You may spill over onto the seat next to you or battle over an armrest, but most of us buy one ticket for our body to fill one seat. Drawing on ideas from Alan Morinis's book *Everyday Holiness*, Rabbi David Jaffe says, "When we say that this seat is mine, we are also saying that that other seat is not mine. By making a set place we are also giving space to others. According to Morinis, this is the key to humility (anavah). The Anavah knows how much space to take up in any situation. When our Anavah is out of balance we take either too little or too much space."[1] It's kind of like our God-given spaces. While we can hold different roles simultaneously, given the boundary lines of time and physical place, we can really only occupy one spot on the planet at a given millisecond. If we aren't listening to God's leading, we could be filling space meant for someone else.

Rightsize to Fill Your Hoop

After drawing up your boundary lines and discerning the space God has assigned you, the next step is to consider whether you need to shrink or swell to fill that space. What adjustments do you need to make? Consider where you spend your time and energy. Do you spend a lot of time concerned with what other people around you are doing? Does comparison cause you envy, jealousy, insecurity? Reading James 3 the other day, I was struck by two phrases: "bitter envy" and "selfish ambition" (v. 14). "Bitter envy" feels like our response when we aren't filling our spaces and we look around, bitter and envious of the courage of others who are. Then "selfish ambition" happens when we overstep our boundaries and pursue things for our own glory and desire for success.

James first warns and then encourages: "For where there is envy and selfish ambition, there will also be disorder and wickedness of every kind. But the wisdom from above is first pure, then peaceable, gentle, willing to yield, full of mercy and good fruits, without a trace of partiality or hypocrisy" (vv. 16–17). Peace, mercy, and good fruit sound way better than disorder and wickedness.

The value in discerning whether a space is God-given or just a good idea is that doing so helps ensure you won't take up space you weren't meant to fill. It helps you confidently own your space and respect where another person's space begins. "Staying in your hoop," as my pastor's wife, Vela, would say. Vela came on my podcast years ago to share the idea of "Hula-Hoop-ology" that her therapist taught her. She said to imagine a Hula-Hoop around you. Everything within the hoop is within your control. Everything outside the hoop isn't. Trouble comes when you or I attempt to manipulate and control the things outside our hoop. Or when we try to get into someone else's hoop. Vela says, "Staying in my Hula-Hoop means accepting God's limits for who I am, where I end, and where another person starts. It means doing what He has called me to do inside my sphere of influence—inside my Hula-Hoop—not meddling in someone else's Hula-Hoop."[2]

It's like the new corporate-structuring concept "rightsizing." While *downsizing* indicates financial trouble and usually includes employee layoffs, *rightsizing* is more about helping a company effectively perform and meet its goals. That could sometimes mean decreasing the number of employees but not always. In a similar way, rightsizing to fill our God-given space is a way to effectively perform in that space and meet the goals God has for us. Rightsizing becomes a moment-to-moment shrinking and swelling to stay in, and fill, our hoops.

Often, we think of humility in vertical terms: being lifted up or brought low. In the book of Isaiah, there is example after example of countries that did not humble themselves to God. But what I find interesting is that the Hebrew word for "pride" in Isaiah 16:6—*ga'on*—is defined as "haughtiness," "arrogance," or even the expansive term "swelling."[3] Taking up more space than allotted. That swelling disrupts not only our relationship with God but also those between ourselves and others. If your goal is to be bigger than those around you, you're not giving them the opportunity to grow with you; you're creating an environment to make them seem small next to you.

Curious to learn more about the Jewish perspective on this concept, I stumbled upon a video series created by Hanan Harchol. Born in Kibbutz Kinneret, Israel, he moved to the United States at the age of two. He now lives in New York as a teacher, filmmaker, animator, artist, and classical guitarist. One of the videos he made was about the Jewish theme of humility. It's an animated conversation between himself and his father in which his father, a wise rabbi, teaches him about the concept of humility. His father uses the imagery of a seed in the ground and points out that as the plant grows, the earth expands to make space. He also uses the example of a baby growing in the womb and points out how the womb expands to accommodate the child taking up more space. The womb and child create together. They stay in "right size" with one another.

"We don't want to take up so much space we squeeze others out or take up so little space that the responsibility falls on others' shoulders."[4] The journey is to expand and contract along the way. Hanan's dad tries to teach him how humility is like the dirt of the earth: the gravitational pull (when we're humble, we draw other people to us), the nourishing aspects (by being humble, we can help ourselves and others grow), and the receiving posture (by making ourselves low, we're in a position to receive and learn from others). "The rabbis create a beautiful wordplay with 'mattanah,' which is both the name of a place and the Hebrew word for 'gift.' If you act with the humility of the wilderness, you will learn more and receive a mattanah. Can you really learn when you are trying to show others how much you know? To go against your nature is strength—to let go of control—being flexible is the strength of humility."[5] Your place becomes a gift when you stay in a posture of receiving, learning, and participating.

Consider the deeper impact we could have on our relationships by allowing others to make their own choices and mistakes and have their own emotions, yet still sympathizing with them and showing them compassion, and by expending our limited amount of time and energy on controlling what is within our ability—our thoughts, emotions, and actions.

Honestly, that list—thoughts, emotions, and actions—most days seems impossible to control. How often do lies cross my mind? Or do my emotions swing reactively? Or do I act in an undesirable way toward those I love? Instead of focusing on filling my mind with truth, reining in my emotions, and loving my people, I often waste my energy trying to tell other people how they should think, feel, and act. Believe me when I tell you that never works out well.

After our church small group worked through the Celebrate Recovery twelve-step program together, I better understood how these three parts of me intertwined and impacted my relationships. It wasn't others (or drugs, alcohol, or shopping) that were the problem. It was a habit of having an emotion, thinking a thought, and responding in a hurtful way. By clueing in to a repeated emotion, I could dig a little deeper into what I was believing and change my reaction. All this work begins with the first step of admitting our limits as humans: what is in our control and what isn't.

The tricky thing within family structures is that our hoops overlap. Parents' hoops overlap with their kids' for so many years, it causes the parents to falsely believe a child's hoop is their hoop. Parents forget to slowly let their children spin their hoops on their own, to gain the skills they need as they fail along the way. This becomes particularly important as we grow to be adults. Vela writes, "Staying out of my kids' hula hoops can be as simple as letting them complete their homework on their own and not jumping in to make the project even better. I also had to learn to stay out of my kids' hula hoops when it concerned bigger issues. At some point, they decide who their friends are, who they date, where/if they go to college, what major to pursue, who they marry, where they live . . . and the list goes on and on. I work hard to give advice only when asked."[6]

Hoop-jumping isn't isolated to our kids. More than once, moms have emailed me asking how they can help their husbands lead their families spiritually. They tell me how they long for their husbands to wholeheartedly love Jesus. I'm confident these women have experienced a lot of spiritual growth through their own time of prayer and Bible study. They're intentional. As moms, they've done a lot of shedding of self over the last few years. But what about their husbands? Who's keeping them accountable? And where are other men to step up and say, "Hey, buddy, you're only thinking about yourself here."

Pastor and author Paul David Tripp answers this question for me in an interview.

> You've got to be careful that you don't have a selfish way of dealing with selfishness. So, you're demanding and critical because that person's selfishness messes up your life? That's never going to produce good stuff in your marriage. That produces arguments and defensiveness. So, I have to say, What is the reason for my concern for my husband? Is it just that I seem to be working harder than he does? Is it just that he makes my life uncomfortable? Or—fasten your seatbelt here—do I look at him like God looks at him and want what is best for him? And this is not best for him. You see, once you're there, then you ask the question, How can I be, as a wife, part of what God wants to do in the life of my husband? And shockingly, this is so counterintuitive.[7]

He goes on to say, "The Bible tells us it's 'the kindness of God that leads us to repentance.' The grace, love, trust, and understanding I bring into a marriage [all within my hoop] draws my husband to Jesus. [Your husband] begins to not need to defend himself in front of you anymore because what he gets from you is grace and not judgment."[8]

Just swap out the word *husband* with *friend* and apply his advice. Because I've seen this dynamic play out between women. The conflict and drama that result from one friend judging another friend's actions. Making assumptions about her motivations. The classic faithful volunteer who turns up her nose because another gal plays tennis instead of helping at the church. The problem isn't that one woman chooses to serve others and one chooses to play on the tennis court (or work in a cubicle or socialize at brunch). The root issue is that one person decides her choice is right and the other's is wrong. One feels she is being responsible and the other is selfish. Negative emotions creep in and disrupt the relationship.

I had the privilege of attending a university that championed servant leadership. At commencement, each graduate received not only a diploma but also a towel. A symbol of Jesus's choice to wash twelve sets of dirty toes the night before He went to the cross. Christ's priority remained in place even if those around Him didn't choose the same. He didn't waste time trying to go outside His hoop and make others choose the same priorities. He spoke the truth of who the Father was and the kingdom He desired to bring to earth. He invited others to simply follow Him.

How vastly different would our communities be if we came alongside one another? Choosing to be a servant leader and inviting others to do the same. Dropping the anger if someone is unable or unwilling to serve. Trusting that God is at work in each of us, making us new day by day. Giving more space for the Holy Spirit to work through each of us in our designated place. And letting the Spirit move in our space as well. I wonder if sometimes the reason we hoop-jump is because it's easier to tell others what to do and how to manage their lives than it is to come face-to-face with our own insecurities and fears.

What about the Giants?

God promised land, a physical God-given space, to His people. He provided for them when famine forced them out of that land. Then He freed them from slavery to return to Israel. Before the Israelites fill that space, the Lord tells Moses to send men, one from each tribe, to scope out Canaan, the promised land. If you attended children's church or Sunday school in the 1980s, do you remember the song based on this story?

> Twelve men went to spy out Canaan.
> (Ten were bad, two were good.)
> What do you think they saw in Canaan?
> (Ten were bad, two were good.)
> Some saw giants, big and tall!
> Some saw grapes in clusters fall.
> Some saw God was in it all.
> (Ten were bad, two were good.)

While I find the good/bad distinction incorrect (we are all sinners and fall short of the glory of God), the point of the song is to demonstrate that twelve men explore the same space. They all agree that the land is fruitful, flowing with milk and honey. But a majority find the people in the land to be intimidating.

> But Caleb [one of the two spies who disagreed] quieted the people before Moses and said, "Let us go up at once and occupy it, for we are well able to overcome it." Then the men who had gone up with him said, "We are not able to go up against this people, for they are stronger than we." (Num. 13:30–31)

The passage goes on to describe giants, the Anakites, who are descendants of the Nephilim (half god/half human). The Israelites weep all night, disappointed to have gone on this long journey only to have to turn back. Joshua tries to encourage them:

> The land that we went through as spies is an exceedingly good land. If the Lord is pleased with us, he will bring us into this land and give it to us, a land that flows with milk and honey. Only, do not rebel against the Lord, and do not fear the people of the land, for they are no more than bread for us; their protection is removed from them, and the Lord is with us; do not fear them. (14:7–9)

They respond to Joshua by wanting to stone him. Nice. They have been set free from Egyptian slavery, fed food from heaven, provided water from a rock, and yet they do not believe God is capable of delivering them into the space He's promised. So they shrink back in fear. Attack the ones who offer comfort. Remain terrified to fill the space God has assigned them.

This kind of shrinking is different from the rightsizing—pulling back from overstepping into someone else's space—that I talked about earlier. What I see most often are individuals who have been given talent, opportunity, and experiences but who don't step into the places God's assigned them because of fear. They're intimidated by the giants in the land. They struggle to believe the God who brought them to that place will strengthen and sustain them. They ultimately miss out on the good things God has prepared for them to do.

The consequence for the Israelites' unbelief is forty years of wandering in the wilderness. Most of them never set foot in the promised land. But Caleb and Joshua, the two who "saw God was in it all," would lead the people at the right time to fill the space God had assigned them.

The book of Joshua begins with familiar encouragement: "Be strong and courageous; do not be frightened or dismayed, for the LORD your God is with you wherever you go" (Josh. 1:9). There is nowhere you can go where God is not with you. And as a believer in Christ's death and resurrection, you carry God in you.

Whenever the topic of this book comes up in conversation, the person I'm talking to shares a space they feel prompted to fill. Out of curiosity (and for book research), I often ask, "What's keeping you from taking the next step?" Typically, the reason comes down to fear. Fear of rejection. Fear of failure. Fear of unknowns. After acknowledging the fear, I then lean in and push into the fear. "What would happen if you did the thing you feel led to do and no one liked it? What would happen next? And then what would happen?"

I basically ask them to name their giants. Frequently, these imagined worst-case-scenario giants shrink when we label them.

I can relate to letting fear hold you back. While I was helping a friend sell earrings at a Christian conference, Jana Burson started a conversation with me. We had a mutual friend, Kat Armstrong, one of the authors she represented. Yep, Jana is a literary agent. While it had been more than five years since my failed attempt at writing a book proposal, I still feared entering that space. I had found my groove with my podcast. Why would I attempt to do something intimidating, hard, unknown?

When the idea of working on a book resurfaced, I had to ask myself those same questions: *What's the worst that would happen if I attempted to write another book proposal and it wasn't good enough to pitch to publishers?* Besides my pride being a bit hurt, honestly, not much would happen. No one but my close friends and family and Jana would even know I tried. *What would happen if we did finish the proposal and no one wanted to publish the book?* Well, then I would have gotten farther in the book-writing process than I had previously. And I would be able to comfort myself knowing that if God desires for me to write a book, He will make it clear. Or that maybe He has something else for me to do (like He did with podcasting). *What if I got the book deal, wrote the book, and everyone hated it?* I would cry, be embarrassed, and never leave my house again. Just kidding. Hopefully I would remember that my identity comes from being a child of God. And my goal is to use the gifts He's given me as best I can. Then leave the results to Him. If people hate what I make, that's on Him (winky face).

Leaving the results to God makes me think of Jesus's miracle when He fed the five thousand. Dallas Jenkins, the creator of the popular *Chosen* series, heard God encourage him to let go of the burden of performance after a failed movie release when he received this comment from a Facebook friend: "Remember, your job is not to feed the 5000. It's only to provide the loaves and fish."[9] To put a spin on his analogy, I don't want to offer rotten fish and moldy loaves. Sometimes filling your God-given space means offering the best of what you have.

The other day I saw the story of an Uber Eats driver who went above and beyond what was expected. He honored the people who'd ordered via the app by carefully placing down tissue paper before leaving their bag of two hot dogs.[10] He also left a gift bag with masks and a poem to bless these customers. There is more freedom and less fear when you and I put energy into doing our best to fill the space God has assigned us and then trust Him with the results and the multiplying. Once the fears are identified and courage rises up, the next step is to take the next step.

Stretching Marks

Another option after we identify our God-given spaces is to settle into a place of "fine." Yes, we feel led to create that thing or start that organization or step into that space. But we may drag our feet, never activating our gifts or talents where we are, for such a time as this, because we're drawn to comfort and convenience.

Choosing the "eating chips on the couch" life sounds awfully appealing. I adore chips and salsa. But I don't believe that's the ultimate reason why God gave me life. Yes, there are healing spaces, grieving spaces, spaces of waiting. But I'm talking about the times when we choose not to move forward because it's difficult or painful.

Taking that first step requires that we prioritize it as being important. Do I believe God is directing me to a particular space? Do I feel like my offering will encourage and bless others and help them better understand the Good News? Then I need to figure out what's my next right step. And then invite others in to keep me accountable.

Paul took steps into his assigned spaces, especially uncomfortable ones. He writes,

> You yourselves know how I lived among you the entire time from the first day that I set foot in Asia, serving the Lord with all humility

and with tears, enduring the trials that came to me through the plots of the Jews. I did not shrink from doing anything helpful. . . . And now, as a captive to the Spirit, I am on my way to Jerusalem, not knowing what will happen to me there, except that the Holy Spirit testifies to me in every city that imprisonment and persecutions are waiting for me. But I do not count my life of any value to myself, if only I may finish my course and the ministry that I received from the Lord Jesus, to testify to the good news of God's grace. (Acts 20:18–20, 22–24)

He knows pain, death, and trials are waiting for him, but he doesn't shrink back to a comfortable spot, eating gelato on the Italian coast. He follows the Spirit's leading and continues to go and make disciples wherever he is assigned to go.

There was a decade when my body felt like an accordion. Every two years, I'd grow a tiny human, my abdomen swelling and stretching to make space for each new life. I always preferred the full, tight pregnant belly to the doughy postpartum one.

It also amazed me how quickly my belly expanded for each pregnancy after the first. Of course, it makes logical sense. The skin had been stretched once before, so there was less resistance to do it again. But that first time was a doozy. My skin itched. I layered on vitamin E oil, praying it would somehow send the message, "Get ready, epithelium; you're gonna need to multiply quickly. There's a nine-pound baby growing in there."

Despite my best efforts and skin pep talks, the stretching left marks. On my hips. That's right; I focused my stretching support on the area with obvious growth but forgot about how my whole body was changing. Now I have permanent evidence to testify. Not just evidence on my body but also with the legacy growing before my eyes in our home. Bruce calls me "The Matriarch." He has three sisters, his dad has four sisters, and his grandfather is an only child. The MacFadyen family tree was a straight line until our family grew four boy offshoots. Four future men to create their own branches. Generations to come, all starting from my stretching accordion belly.

Sometimes an assignment requires us to stretch beyond what's comfortable. We need to believe the hard parts will be worth it for our future life and legacy. Like Isaiah writes to the Israelites, addressing them as a childless wife, "Enlarge the site of your tent, and let the curtains of your habitations be stretched out; do not hold back; lengthen your cords and strengthen your stakes" (Isa. 54:2). He's reminding them that even though the current state is seemingly empty, like a barren womb, it is time to expand their homes and stretch out their tents because a multiplication is coming. After Christ's birth, death, and resurrection, those who belong to the kingdom of heaven will stretch beyond the Israelites to the gentiles. It is a message of hope to create the space for God to do the growing.

It may be your first year of marriage. Or a move to a new community. Or the launch of your dream business. All these spaces require that you endure an uncomfortable stage in order to fill the space you're being assigned. But then you look back and realize the stretching marked you. What was once so intimidating is doable—maybe not easy, but you've experienced doing it once before. Confidence comes from pushing through the hard. You aren't the same as you once were.

My friend Courtney DeFeo is the ultimate cheerleader and connector. If someone she knows deserves celebrating, you better believe she's bringing balloons. What I appreciate about my friend is how her painful stretching actually happened in occupying a smaller space.

Both Courtney and her husband, Ron, held prominent leadership positions at a global PR firm. As time went on, Courtney and Ron had two gorgeous girls and moved into different careers. Courtney began writing, speaking, and creating family-culture resources, while Ron moved into various corporate positions. Eventually his roles required more time and energy, and she realized for their family to function the way she desired, she needed to pull back some of the work she was doing outside the home. While that was a challenging decision, she felt God's leading and assurance in it.

At the end of 2021, Ron was promoted to senior vice president and chief communications officer for American Airlines. When he was given the role, his boss, who was retiring, took the time to encourage Courtney with these words: "You are a force of nature behind Ron. You took a step back so he could take a step forward."

While Courtney loves being a stay-at-home mom, she is also an achiever. When she and Ron were peers working at the global PR firm, Courtney had dreams of being a CEO one day. So receiving words of acknowledgment in her choice to fill a seemingly smaller space than she had imagined filling gave her the boost she needed to keep going.

Though there is a stretching required when we're filling a space we've been hesitant to fill, we have to recognize we are human *beings*, not human *doings*. In the uncomfortable places, we have to lean more on God. As we take on risks, we become desperately dependent on God for each moment.

The ultimate rightsized life verse is, "Come to me, all you who are weary and are carrying heavy burdens, and I will give you rest. Take my yoke upon you, and learn from me, for I am gentle and humble in heart, and you will find rest for your souls. For my yoke is easy, and my burden is light" (Matt. 11:28–30). A yoke was a beam that coupled two working animals together. This is Jesus's way of saying, "Be connected to Me as your way of finding balance." He becomes our rightsizing guide. The fantastic thing about Jesus being the measure of workload is that the load can be different for each person and each season and each moment.

DISCUSSION QUESTIONS

1. Do you struggle with staying inside your Hula-Hoop? Whose hoop are you tempted to jump in most often?

2. How would your relationships be impacted if you focused your time and energy on your own thoughts, emotions, and actions?

3. Do you need to shrink or swell to rightsize yourself in your God-given space?

4. What are the names of the giants keeping you from fully occupying your God-given space?

5. What uncomfortable stretching do you need to push through as you trust God for the outcomes?

Tending Your Space

However many years she lived, Mary always felt that "she should never forget that first morning when her garden began to grow."

Frances Hodgson Burnett, *The Secret Garden*

Confession: I can be confident that God is assigning me to a space and at the same time question the assignment if it requires setting boundaries on other areas of my family life. If leading a conference, praying with a friend, serving on a community board, taking dinner to a family in crisis, or replying to emails means I have to say no to being with my kids, there's an inner tug-of-war.

I forget that I'm important but not essential to the good plans God has for my kids. While the goal is not to neglect the needs of my children, I tend to fall to the other extreme and feel guilty about choosing to take time away to work on a project God has assigned me. The feeling of guilt typically means I believe I'm doing something wrong. When I peel back the layers on why I feel it's wrong not to be 100 percent available to my children, it comes down to ownership. Instead of believing my children are a gift from God to be stewarded, I believe they were created by me and that I am the keeper of their destinies. This doesn't just apply to our kids. With our careers or our ministries, we may think we own the spaces and have created our mini-kingdoms to rule. And in the process, we forget that we are merely stewards of the spaces we're assigned.

Trapping Foxes

At the start of the new year, I was curious to hear what words people had selected as their words of the year, so I posed the question in my Instastory. After collecting several entries, I shared the list. A moment later, a gal direct-messaged me, saying, "You didn't include mine." At first I was annoyed at her attention to detail. It had taken me a good thirty minutes to type all the words into a document. She happened to notice I had missed hers. The nerve!

Then I did a little digging to find the word of the year she'd sent me. Once I found it, I remembered why I had skipped it. "Foxes." She'd written "foxes." So I messaged her back: "I'm so sorry. I saw your word, but I thought it was mistyped or maybe a joke because one of my friends, trying to be funny, wrote 'mariachi band.' I'd love to know more about your word."

She sent me laughing emojis and then an explanation:

I never get a word of the year. But I just kept thinking about foxes. I have actually never seen a fox until moving to Scotland. Then earlier last year we had a fox in our garden and I was really freaked out to see it climb right under our bedroom window into some hedges. Usually I don't think of them fondly but then I kept coming across images of them and thinking how cool and beautiful they looked. So finally I looked them up in my Bible and came across: "Catch all the foxes, those little foxes, before they ruin the vineyard of love, for the grapevines are blossoming!" (Song of Sol. 2:15 NLT). At first I was looking at it in regards to my marriage. But then I felt the Holy Spirit telling me it was about me and Jesus. I've been wanting to feel and be closer to him. I felt like it was a word to not let whatever these foxes are get in the way of my walk with the Lord. My goal this year is to not let these things compete with my affection for the Lord. So whenever I think or hear of foxes, it reminds me of that. Keep Jesus my Lord. Keep Hope alive. And not get distracted or discouraged by what's going on around me in the natural world.

Wow! And to think I almost skipped having this interaction because I dismissed her word and was annoyed at her pointing out my error.

What's even more amazing is the fox theme didn't stop with her message. I decided to share her words (with permission) and ask others for examples of how "foxes" steal from their intimacy with God. Some of their responses were "noise," "constant commitments," "comparison," "my iPhone," "social media," "pride," "laziness," "distraction," and "high expectations." Have you considered what would be on your list? What things are actively stealing from your future fruitfulness in your assigned space?

Next, I asked for thoughts on how to keep these "foxes" from impacting intimacy with Jesus. A gal sent me this story:

> I looked out my back door yesterday to see two foxes had cornered my cat and looked like they were going to attack and kill her. The situation looked very ominous and their eyes had an evil intent. But here's another analogy for you. The minute I walked outside and yelled and clapped my hands they ran away scared. All it took was me clapping my hands for these carnivores to go running. They seemed like they were about to cause destruction and a simple act sent them running. There's a sermon in that.

There certainly is. I'd call that scattering technique a "holy clap."

Yes, there are natural distractions to our fruitfulness, but there are also supernatural ones. But a holy clap empowered by the Spirit of God can send them running. Personally, this has looked like praying out loud, "Be gone in the name of Jesus Christ, the Lamb who was slain. You are not welcome here. Be cast to the foot of the cross, never to return again." There is a supernatural battle at hand. Too often we forget the truth that we have been equipped with authority in the spaces we occupy.

Active Sabotage

In tending our God-given spaces, not only do we have to expose external threats, but we also have to be on alert to some internal ones. Like I shared in chapter 1, believing a lie like "I'm missing out" steals my peace. Wrong thinking patterns can actively work against me, creating false narratives about my situation.

For me that looks like giving the enemy headspace and letting him influence my thoughts. Especially when I say yes to following God into the spaces He's assigned me. What's tricky is that the way the enemy often works is through thought processes that may have worked for me in the past. Neurologists have discovered that we have a portion of our brain that helps us calmly problem-solve, be patient, and learn. One author, Shirzad Chamine, calls this our "positive intelligence." The goal is to use this portion of our brain a majority of the time. Unfortunately, because of past experiences and coping strategies, we have thinking patterns, or what Chamine calls "saboteurs," that disrupt our positive intelligence.

Based on research, Chamine identifies one master saboteur, the judge, that "beats you up repeatedly over mistakes or shortcomings, warns you obsessively about future risks, wakes you up in the middle of the night worrying, gets you fixated on what is wrong with others or your life, etc. Your Judge activates your other Saboteurs, causes much of your stress and unhappiness, reduces your effectiveness, and harms your relationships."[1] Chamine determines there are ten total potential saboteurs: judge, avoider, controller, hyper-achiever, hyper-rational, hyper-vigilant, pleaser, restless, stickler, and victim.[2]

I took his online test and discovered my top five saboteurs are hyper-achiever, restless, pleaser, hyper-vigilant, and victim. Another assessment revealed that I spend 68 percent of my time listening to these saboteurs—68 percent! That's a lot of mental space working against the good God has for me.

The hyper-achiever tells me that love is conditional based on performance. The restless saboteur keeps me unsettled in my current place, seeking excitement and contentment in the next thing. My pleaser tries to fulfill my deep emotional needs for acceptance and belonging through helping others and saying what I think they want to hear. The hyper-vigilant saboteur causes continuous anxiety about what could go wrong next. And the victim wants to give up and withdraw when things get hard or I feel misunderstood.

Y'all, listing these out is incredibly eye-opening. I can see how each one has been at work to keep me from writing the words in this very book. How many other assigned God-given spaces have I allowed the enemy to sabotage with similar lies? In an automated email based on my assessment results, Chamine pointed out that "the first step in weakening your Saboteurs is to identify and expose them, as you can't fight an invisible enemy, or one pretending to be your friend." Labeling the lie and holding it out in full view helps us defeat it.

When one of these saboteurs tries to take me off course, I address it: "Thank you, hyper-achiever, for helping me succeed to this point. But you can step down. I know my value and worth come from Christ alone. Performance will never make me more lovable than I already am." I address these lies with a voice of grace and compassion, understanding where they came from but also intentionally redirecting my attention to truth.

Tear Down High Places

Most children's Bibles include the story of David and Goliath. I vaguely remember a flannel-board presentation of David's son

Solomon becoming king and helping two moms who were arguing over a baby. But I'm confident no Sunday school teacher taught me about King Rehoboam, Solomon's son, and how his harsh policies led to the revolt of the northern tribes and the division of Israel. Or about how when it was divided, Rehoboam ruled over the tribes of Judah, and Jeroboam, a servant's son, ruled over Israel.

Throughout 1 and 2 Kings, the kings are described as following either the way of David or the sins of Jeroboam. They either did right or did evil in the eyes of the Lord. Some kings chose a combination of these options: followed the ways of David but did wrong in the eyes of the Lord, or did what was right but "the high places were not removed." But what are "high places"? With 117 mentions in the Old Testament, we know they played a significant role in biblical culture.

Before God gave the promised land to the Israelites, the Canaanites occupied it. Once the Israelites settled into the land, the Canaanites lived around the nation of Israel and worshiped other gods. In addition to temples built to Baal (the god of agriculture and fertility), they constructed "high places," often positioned on a hill above town, with a seat for the deity and an Asherah pole (wooden post) to mark the place sacred. By sacrificing to the gods who controlled agricultural fertility and fruitfulness, they hoped to control the outcome of their harvests.

Before we judge this practice, perhaps you and I should consider how we similarly try to manipulate favorable and fruitful outcomes in our God-given spaces. We may not be as archaic as the Canaanites (or the Israelites) and sacrifice our children on an altar. Or do we? This may look like sacrificing rest and family connection by signing up for extra sports in the name of possible college scholarships (financial fruitfulness and trophy children). Or we might sacrifice time in God's Word to type out a few more emails in the morning in an attempt to control work success. Perhaps we sacrifice fellowship with friends because we are "too busy," but we make time to spend an hour scrolling through Instagram, longing for approval and connection with influencers (social fruitfulness).

The questions to ask ourselves are, *What places of idol worship am I allowing to remain in this God-given space? What am I giving my time, attention, and energy to in hopes that I can control the outcome? What am I believing is a better god to serve?* In answering those questions, a helpful prayer comes from Psalm 139:

> Examine me, O God, and probe my thoughts.
> Test me, and know my concerns.
> See if there is any idolatrous way in me,
> and lead me in the everlasting way. (vv. 23–24 NET)

Be a Priest

In the book of Numbers, Moses gives the Israelites clear instructions on how they are to occupy the land, including what they are to do with the high places. He says, "Destroy all their figured stones, destroy all their cast images, and demolish all their high places" (Num. 33:52). Thirty kings fail to remove high places. They are convinced keeping them is better than destroying them. However, one king, Hezekiah, doesn't just tear down the Baal temples and high places, he replaces them with temples to worship the Lord.

At just twenty-five years old, King Hezekiah chooses to undo the horrible things of his father, King Ahaz. He notes that his ancestors have "shut the doors of the portico and put out the lamps. They did not burn incense or present any burnt offerings at the sanctuary to the God of Israel" (2 Chron. 29:7 NIV). They have put out the fires. They haven't been honoring or worshiping God. In the first month of his first year as king, Hezekiah opens the temple doors, which his dad had nailed shut. He not only opens the temple but also brings in priests and instructs them to consecrate and restore the temple for worship.

When we've done the tending work to tear down high places, trap sneaky foxes, and call out saboteurs, we then have a choice about what to put in their place. This process requires a heart posture that desires to increase in faith and intimacy with God. You can be in an assigned space, minus the high places, but not invite God to help you make the space sacred (a.k.a. "consecrated"). With our belief in Christ's death and resurrection, you and I carry the presence of God in us. We become walking temples (see 1 Cor. 6:19). While it was the job of the priests to care for the temple, and the high priest to enter the most Holy of Holies once a year to keep the incense burning, it is now our job to be the priests of the temple, which is our God-given space: ourselves. We create the rhythms to foster a consecrated spiritual experience.

Paul reminds his mentee Timothy to "rekindle the gift of God that is within you through the laying on of my hands, for God did not give us a spirit of cowardice but rather a spirit of power and of love and of self-discipline" (2 Tim. 1:6–7). Rekindle the gift within you. Faith is not a once-and-done experience. *Rekindle* means to relight. As Paul reminds Timothy, the relighting process empowered by the Holy Spirit includes self-discipline, which, by the way, we don't have to muster! If, like me, you struggle to keep structure in your life, then ask God to fill you with a spirit of self-discipline. He not only empowers us but can inspire us to implement structure and spiritual rhythms to keep our faith fires going.

In the early church, after Constantine legalized Christianity, believers went to the desert to nurture their connection with God. They first went as hermits and then they gathered in communities. The concept of monasteries was born. These groups gathered around a set of practices to help maintain their dependence on God. In AD 397, Augustine wrote a "rule of common life" for lay Christians. The word *rule* here isn't a set of regulations. It is more synonymous with the concept of a trellis, to stick with the garden metaphor. If we think of the sneaky foxes stealing from our future fruitfulness, we could think of a rule of life as a structure that anchors and allows for growth. A rule of life provides the support for us to abide in Christ and experience growth in our God-given spaces.

In tending our spaces, we become gardeners or farmers. Concerned less with what is going on with the crop next to us, we are more focused on providing the right conditions for growth on our land.

> Be patient, therefore, brothers and sisters, until the coming of the Lord. The farmer waits for the precious crop from the earth, being patient with it until it receives the early and the late rains. You also must be patient. Strengthen your hearts, for the coming of the Lord is near. (James 5:7–8)

Our part is to be patient and strengthen our hearts, trusting God for the future harvest and fruitfulness. (Remember, the "fruit" is of the Spirit, not our efforts.) How do we create a rule of life to consistently abide in Christ and allow our hearts to be strengthened? There are loads and loads of guides to help us do this. Ancient options and very cute trendy ones. Simple and complex.

On a recent Sunday, our small group had a pastor friend, Matt Klingler, join us. He shared that he recently implemented a daily rule of life. In a simple journal, he writes on three topics in the morning: (1) *Commit Life*—he praises who God is, which leads Matt to commit his life in devotion to Him; (2) *Submit Plans*—he resigns his plans to God, gives God permission to change them, and asks for God's presence and his own obedience with those changes; (3) *Accept Grace*—he preemptively accepts God's grace for his disobedience and shortcomings.

Then in the evening, he reflects on three topics: (1) *Rejoice*—he writes out his gratitude for what went well; (2) *Repent*—he confesses where he needs correction and to go God's way; and (3) *Receive*—he accepts anything God's showing, teaching, or telling him that day.

My hope is that if you have no spiritual rhythm to your day, you can implement Matt's rule of life. Simple enough to execute and gracious enough not to have to do every day. But intentional enough to impact your God-given space.

There are also options that are a bit more complex. Every year, my friend Angela and I meet to help each other work through our in-depth, goal-planning journals. I've come to realize these journals are a rule-of-life tool. The process helps me evaluate the past year and ask God what He would like to cultivate in my life the next year. Verbalizing my rule of life creates clear boundaries on my space: what to say yes to and what is an automatic no.

To be honest, at the beginning of 2022, I started brainstorming and evaluating my life but never wrote out goals. I realized I had been living out my rule of life; it just wasn't explicitly stated. My primary space to occupy was caring for my immediate family—connecting in the morning before school, supporting them in the afternoon with rides/homework/processing, and regular family meals around the table. I had daily and weekly connection points in place with Bruce—praying together in the kitchen before he left for work, taking Saturday morning walks, and weekly date nights. My next most pressing priority was work—producing weekly podcast episodes, keeping listeners engaged through social media, and writing my second book.

In order to stay centered in the Spirit, I also had the rhythms of daily time in prayer and God's Word and weekly time in corporate worship and teaching. For the first quarter of the year, I had to say no to lunches with friends, midday Bible studies, and fun dance classes. Time with friends had shifted to evenings and weekends in order to focus daytime energy on the other four areas (family, spouse, work, and faith). Making time for fun Netflix shows or painting by number also had to happen less often. You and I only have twenty-four hours in a day. There are seasons when we need tighter rules of life to fill our God-given spaces.

It's your God-given space. Own it like you would a garden. Be ruthless to dig up what isn't working. Build fences to keep out sneaky foxes. And plant the things that fire you up. Follow your passion and see where it leads. The word *passion* comes from the Latin root word *pati*, which means "to suffer."

I love this quote from my 2022 Cultivate What Matters planner: "To live your passion means to live wholeheartedly for something worthwhile, knowing all good pursuits cost us something. When you live your passion, making bold decisions and enduring challenges is worth it." Following a passion can require sacrifice. Just as the sacrifices in the temple were an act of worship, our daily choices and sacrifices to manage our time, energy, and resources in order to honor God are acts of worship. However, God is clear that going through the motions of sacrifice without faithfulness is a waste. "The sacrifice God desires is a *humble* spirit" (Ps. 51:17 NET, emphasis added). He desires the sacrifice of fully occupying your God-given space.

Like priests managing the temple, we have been given the responsibility of stewardship to carefully tend our spaces. And maybe for you that includes naming what needs attention. Creating a purposeful plan for daily/weekly/monthly/annual habits to relight the passion in your life. In the past, maybe you've nailed the temple doors shut. You've let the incense burn out. Foxes distracted you and robbed your future fruitfulness. Or maybe saboteurs are telling you lies to keep you from using your positive intelligence and to keep you terrified of the giants in the land. The story isn't over.

DISCUSSION QUESTIONS

1. What "foxes" are currently stealing from your future fruitfulness? How do you analogously "scare them away" or "capture them"?

2. How have you experienced unhelpful thought patterns that distract you from your God-given space? Share some of your common "saboteurs."

3. What occupies a majority of your time, energy, and attention? Have you considered how those things (even church-related) could become high places or idols in your life?

4. What is your experience with "rule of life" practices? Do you have habits or rhythms in your day/week/month that foster personal growth?

5. If you have a journal handy, write down my friend Matt's three morning-prayer focuses (*Commit Life*, *Submit Plans*, and *Accept Grace*) and his three evening-prayer focuses (*Rejoice*, *Repent*, and *Receive*). Try praying through them one day this week. What was your experience? How did the intentional time of prayer impact your day?

Wherever You Go

There are no "ifs" in God's world. And no places that are safer than other places. The center of His will is our only safety ... let us pray that we may always know it!

Corrie ten Boom

There used to be a myth in Christian parenting circles that shepherds broke their sheep's legs to keep them from going wayward. This false analogy started in a book titled *What Jesus Said* by Robert Boyd Munger published in 1955. It was then used in a sermon illustration by William Marrion Branham called "The Good Shepherd of Sheep." There is no scriptural or extrabiblical support of this shepherding technique. In fact, it would be financially unwise to injure a sheep. Not to mention the predatory risk to the whole flock if a shepherd had to carry a seventy-five-pound sheep for six to twelve weeks while the leg healed.[1]

Studying this further, I learned the difference between a sheepherder and a shepherd. A sheepherder drives the flock from behind, while a shepherd leads from the front, and their sheep follow. There are differences not only in how sheep are moved but in how the person interacts with the animals. A sheepherder is a hired hand who has no ownership of the long-term welfare of the sheep, who may abandon the sheep if met with danger, who relies on intimidation and pain to keep sheep moving in the right direction, and who may force sheep into dangerous terrain that can't be seen from the back of the flock. On the other hand, a shepherd proactively shows a sheep how to avoid dangers and obstacles, assumes responsibility for the sheep's long-term welfare, and relies on a trusting relationship to lead them on the best path.

In John 10:27 Jesus says, "My sheep hear my voice. I know them, and they *follow* me" (emphasis added). Jesus sounds like a lead-from-the-front kind of shepherd. In a post about the theology of the Good Shepherd, David and Amanda Erickson point out, "Sheep are so intimately attuned to the shepherd's voice that two herds can be grazing together and if one shepherd calls out his herd, only his sheep will come to him. They know and deeply trust their shepherd. Breaking their legs would definitely break that deep and abiding trust."[2] Not only does Jesus lead us on our way, He's a trustworthy guide.

As I go along on my way, like I shared in an earlier chapter, having a God-listening heart helps guide me in which space to fill next. Since life is a series of occupying various God-given spaces, the journey through those spaces requires tuning my soul to listen to the voice of God. The shepherd David understood this relationship when he wrote,

> I bless the LORD, who gives me counsel. . . .
> I keep the LORD always before me. . . .
> You show me the path of life.
> In your presence there is fullness of joy. (Ps. 16:7–8, 11)

Thinking of shepherds also brings to mind Psalm 23. Yes, God leads us to green pastures, by still waters, to right paths. But in this psalm, David acknowledges how part of the journey is through a valley blanketed with death's shadow. Even in those dark places, because of God's presence, David doesn't fear the evil around him. In the presence of David's enemies, God anoints his head with oil. This anointing acts as further confirmation not to fear. At that time, anointing served as a way of assigning a future God-given space.

At fifteen years old, David is assigned by God, through the prophet Samuel, to lead the people of Israel as king. Before he sees that reality, he spends years hiding and fleeing King Saul's murder attempts. David knows he has been chosen by God for that assigned space, but his day-to-day reality falls short. He waits fifteen years before he fills the space on the throne. The valley of the shadow of death is a long route in his journey.

David's son Solomon writes, "The way of the LORD is a stronghold for the upright" (Prov. 10:29). The Hebrew word for "way" is *derek*, and it's used 705 times in Scripture to describe one's journey, life, direction, or path.[3] If you follow the Lord's direction, that path becomes a stronghold or place of refuge. Wherever following the Lord takes you, you are soul secure. That's not a promise of protection from suffering, but it is knowing that "whoever walks in integrity walks securely" (v. 9).

The word *integrity* here means "completeness" or "full."[4] To walk fully, to fully occupy the way, the path, the spaces God aligns for you, is to walk securely. That word *securely* comes from the Hebrew word *betakh*, which means "a place of refuge, assurance, confidence, and hope."[5] So, we could interpret this proverb to read, "Whoever fully occupies each space on their journey will journey in confident safety." But what about those times of suffering? The spaces that feel less like a place of refuge or comfort and more like a prison?

One Remaining Freedom

While standing in her garage, reviewing the day's plans, suddenly my friend Cari could no longer see her husband even though her eyes were open. To add to her challenge, a massive snowstorm had shut down Dallas for the previous few days and had led to busted pipes and no electricity. Thankfully, the roads were clear enough and the hospital close enough that they were able to get there and figure out what was going on in Cari's body. Unfortunately, an MRI revealed gray polka dots on her brain and spine, evidence that her body had been fighting. Based on the neurology, doctors handed my friend Cari a diagnosis of multiple sclerosis.

A month later, I sat in Cari's living room, held her hands, and with full confidence said, "You haven't been benched. This is an assignment, not a disqualification." I knew her heart's desire to minister, teach, and guide others to know God more fully. Enrolled at the time at the Dallas Theological Seminary, Cari sacrificed time and energy to go deeper in on the things of God so she could shine a light more brightly. While she was hopeful to teach and lead others into the glorious, good news of Jesus, she found herself in the prison of not knowing if her legs would carry her across the room, let alone hold her up on a stage.

In Genesis, we read about Joseph, who has literal dreams of holding a powerful position, with his father and brothers bowing down to him. Whether it is his pompous attitude, his father's favoritism, or his brothers' jealousy, those dreams lead his brothers to sell Joseph as a slave. After serving in an Egyptian palace and being wrongly accused, Joseph lands in prison. He has a choice about how he can respond to this reality. How will he spend his time in prison? He could play the role of victim and brood over his brothers' betrayal. Or he could stay embittered about being falsely accused by Potiphar's wife. Joseph chooses neither. "But the Lord was with Joseph and showed him steadfast love; he gave him favor in the sight of the chief jailer" (Gen. 39:21). In that God-given prison space, Joseph uses his gifts and his experiences, empowered by God, to interpret dreams right where he is.

As a psychiatrist, and from his three years in a Nazi concentration camp, Viktor Frankl offers invaluable perspective and insights on suffering. In his bestselling book *Man's Search for Meaning*, Frankl writes, "Everything can be taken from a man but one thing: the last of the human freedoms—to choose one's attitude in any given set of circumstances, to choose one's own way."[6] He believed that once you find meaning in what you are going through, you are no longer suffering. So, instead of being a victim of his circumstances, he chose to see the purpose.

> Suddenly I saw myself standing on the platform of a well-lit, warm and pleasant lecture room. In front of me sat an attentive audience on comfortable upholstered seats. I was giving a lecture on the psychology of the concentration camp! All that oppressed me at that moment became objective, seen and described from the remote viewpoint of science. By this method I succeeded somehow in rising above the situation, above the sufferings of the moment, and I observed them as if they were already of the past. Both I and my troubles became the object of an interesting psychoscientific study undertaken by myself.[7]

In making the choice to take an objective view of his suffering, he survived. In fact, he didn't just survive; his book has sold millions of copies, his words providing hope and direction for so many. He normalized people's abnormal reactions to abnormal circumstances.

I thought I'd share some of his observations with you in case you are in a prison-like space. Frankl notes, "Three phases of the inmate's mental reactions to camp life become apparent: the period following his admission; the period when he is well entrenched in camp routine; and the period following his release and liberation."[8] That first phase is one of shock. If you are in a season of suffering, you may feel the shock of life being very different from how you hoped it would be.

I hope you openly communicate your shock to God, like David does in the Psalms. God is able to handle our raw emotions and our wrestling. We may find ourselves in difficult circumstances and actively blame God for the suffering. When challenging circumstances come, often we may believe God is punishing us. Like in the example of the bad shepherd, we may believe He's breaking us.

In Israel's history, there was a season of bad shepherds, kings who consistently lost their way and led the people astray. Despite God's patient restoration after each cycle of disobedience, the Israelites eventually found themselves exiled from the promised land. This God-given space, promised to them from the time of Abraham, was then taken by another nation. The temple, the location of God's presence, was destroyed. And the people of Israel moved to a new land. A foreign land. Babylon. Talk about shock.

None of us are promised controlled, convenient, comfortable lives. But I had been living as though a perfect life were guaranteed. When suffering arrived, I had to realign my beliefs about who God is outside my space. When grief barged in, I had to choose to go to the very One I blamed for my suffering, trusting that even in the hardest circumstances God knows more than I ever could. He can do more than I can ever imagine, and He cares more than my heart will ever understand.

The Reality of Suffering

Chunks of my mom's hair flew across our back porch as my hand steadily shaved a row at a time. Each pass of the clippers was another reminder of all that cancer had taken from us. A few hours later, I ordered a flower arrangement for my father's casket. A single day in January held activities I hadn't scheduled a month earlier.

My other roles as mom and wife were operating on autopilot while my part as caregiving daughter took over. As I drove my mom to cancer treatments, cared for her through surgery, and did my best to keep her alive, the unresolved grief from my dad's passing hardened inner places of my soul. Unhealthy beliefs about who

God is seeped in unnoticed and went undealt with until I became physically ill myself.

A year later, at what felt like rock bottom, I claimed 2018 as my resurrection year. The "how" of coming back to life remained unknown, but the need of it was made glaringly apparent by none other than a cute puppy named Lucy, who joined our home. This tiny creature flipped a switch in me, unleashing a new level of anxiety, which expressed itself in the secondary emotion of anger. Every time she attacked my youngest son, I felt uncontrollable fear that came out as rage. I didn't know why I reacted that way and had no idea how to change my reaction.

After Lucy had been with us a month, we decided she would be a better fit for another family, and we rehomed her. That began my search for what was going on inside my body. Like I had learned through our church's twelve-step program, actions are rooted in thoughts and expressed in feelings. My emotional response to a puppy did not add up.

I started by seeing a doctor and discovered my body was sick. My stress hormones were too high and my thyroid numbers too low. I risked seizures with drastically low vitamin D. My gut stopped working effectively. The doctor started me on a supplement regimen and regular blood checks. While this started to help with my fatigue, the anger and anxiety remained.

The first week in July, I learned that my high school friend and former bridesmaid had been in a car accident. Her entire family was left unconscious and hospitalized. Within a week, her middle son, only fourteen years old, passed away from complications. The next day, I discovered that a five-year-old girl from my sons' school had been diagnosed with a brain tumor and would undergo surgery.

That Sunday, I headed to family camp at Pine Cove in Tyler, Texas, still burdened by the suffering of friends and unaware of how those scenarios reinforced a lie I'd been believing. The Bible teacher for our week of camp led us through the book of Ruth and the reality of suffering. How timely.

Naomi, Ruth's mother-in-law, was familiar with loss. With the passing of her husband and her two sons, she asked Ruth to call her Mara, which means "bitter." Who wants to be called bitter? Not me. I sat there taking notes, but my pen stopped when our speaker defined bitterness for us with a quote from Tim Keller: "Worry is not believing God will get it right, and bitterness is believing God got it wrong."[9] Ouch. The words resonated with something inside me. God got it wrong. With my dad's passing. Wrong. With caring for my mom through cancer. Wrong. With my friend's teenage son. Wrong. With a sweet little girl's brain. Wrong.

I was bitter. Call me Mara.

Even though Naomi was bitter, Ruth demonstrated unfailing love toward her. The kind of love God shows us repeatedly. Instead of staying in her hometown, a familiar place, Ruth offers to leave with Naomi:

> Do not press me to leave you,
>   to turn back from following you!
> Where you go, I will go;
>   where you lodge, I will lodge;
> your people shall be my people
>   and your God my God. (Ruth 1:16)

God in His mercy doesn't leave us to our false beliefs. He is not afraid of going with you to dig out past wounds. Or in my case, to unearth growing bitterness while in the greenhouse of family camp. A place where the environment is right for growth and healing. He'd surrounded me with good friends who believed in the power of healing prayer. When I shared my enlightenment with them, they immediately offered to pray with me. In a supernatural moment of confession, God removed the root of bitterness. I simply agreed with Him: "Lord, I have been believing that You got it wrong with my dad. Please forgive me." I felt His forgiveness pour over me, and I verbally accepted that forgiveness.

Two days later, in the same room where God made me aware of my wrong belief, my boys and I danced. My heart felt free and happy for the first time in eighteen months. And David's words from Psalm 30:11 rang true: "You have turned my mourning into dancing." He had turned my body from death to life: *resurrection*—my word for 2018. And this life healing came from the very One I had blamed for my pain.

Suffering does that. It creates a division between a broken heart and the Soul Healer, and it disrupts right beliefs about who God is. Our family-camp speaker said that during times of pain we often question "if God can" and "if God cares." Could God have removed the cancer from my dad's liver? If He could and didn't, did God even care about me or my dad? You may have your own places of hurt and find yourself wondering if God can or if He cares.

Scripture repeats this truth of God's character—He can. He is the Creator. As Creator, He is all-powerful over creation. He can split the sea, quiet the storm, and bring the dead to life. His sovereignty is woven throughout the pages of the Bible. In John 11, Mary approaches Jesus and says, "Lord, if you had been here, my brother would not have died" (v. 32). She believes that Jesus, God incarnate, can heal. She also knows Jesus cares, as His tears reveal to the Jews around Him who say, "See how he loved him!" (v. 36).

If we wonder if God cares, John clears it up with these words: "For God so loved the world that he gave his only Son, so that everyone who believes in him may not perish but may have eternal life" (3:16). When we lose loved ones, God knows how that feels. He chose to give up His only Son for us. The best news is that death no longer ends the story. With belief, we gain access to eternity.

My dad started living eternally when he professed his faith in 1963. My eternity started with a simple prayer in a kindergarten classroom in 1982. In God's timeline, the moment of belief begins our forever in His presence.

It was the hope of eternity and my healing at family camp that helped me properly grieve through the tragic death of my friend

Wynter Pitts on July 24, 2018, a mere two weeks after God had removed the seed of bitterness from my heart. On my calendar for July 25 was the event "Farewell Wynter Lunch." You see, even in this tragedy—the loss of a young mom of four girls—God paved the way with grace.

The Pitts family had already bought a house in Nashville. Before officially leaving Dallas, their family would enjoy a week of goodbye celebrations. Wynter's friends had gathered notes telling her how much she'd meant to them. The day before she passed into God's presence, she had read over each note. Each friend had a chance to say goodbye, not knowing her destination was heaven. The stories of God's grace to walk through heartache don't end there. Her legacy lives on in her four precious girls as they maneuver this place between the "already" of salvation and the "not yet" of eternity.

Escape versus Deliverance

David waited fifteen years to be king. Joseph waited two years in prison for the cupbearer to mention him to Pharaoh. The Israelites waited seventy years in exile, wondering when they could return to Jerusalem. My friend Cari waited for her body to be healed. One of the challenges of fully occupying a suffering space is holding on to hope when we have no idea how long the hard will last.

Frankl documents this from his time in the concentration camp:

Psychological observations of the prisoners have shown that only the men who allowed their inner hold on their moral and spiritual selves to subside eventually fell victim to the camp's degenerating influences. The question now arises, what could, or should, have constituted this "inner hold"? Former prisoners, when writing or relating their experiences, agree that the most depressing influence of all was that a prisoner could not know how long his term of imprisonment would be. He had been given no date for his release.[10]

How do we hold on to our spiritual self when we don't know when we'll be set free? One of the coping strategies for hard circumstances is escape. When we don't know when the suffering will end, we craft an escape plan—an attempt to end the suffering. But God calls us to lean on His deliverance—His timing and method—and not to lean on our limited vision and control. Part of me wonders what would happen to our inner hold if the focus shifted from desiring escape to waiting for deliverance. Bolstering our faith in the One outside our space who controls all things. Believing that nothing is impossible. If God created all things, then He has all things at His disposal to deliver us from a particular space at the right time.

Paul and Silas sat in the innermost cell, their feet in stocks. Their crime had been freeing a slave girl from a spirit of divination. Her owners, furious at the loss of income, had cried out for Paul and Silas's arrest. The men had no idea how long they would wait in that prison cell. How do they choose to pass the time? "About midnight Paul and Silas were praying and singing hymns to God, and the prisoners were listening to them" (Acts 16:25).

They are fully occupying their God-given space with prayer and praise. There is no plan of escape. They have been given a platform, even if it is a dirty prison floor, sitting in their own excrement. The space doesn't change their faith, but their faith changes their space.

Paul and Silas know their God sets slaves free; they have just witnessed a girl set free. If it is His will, He will set them free too. With access to all creation at His disposal, God shakes the ground, opens the prison doors, and breaks everyone's chains. But Paul and Silas do not flee. They wait until they are released. A life-and-death decision. I'm not being dramatic either. When the prison doors fly open in the pitch-black of night, the jailer assumes all the prisoners have escaped. He is about to take his own life when Paul yells out, "Do not harm yourself, for we are all here" (v. 28).

Because they have maximized their humble platform, they have faith followers, the first prison ministry. In awe, the jailer asks about salvation for himself. And his whole family follows. Generations are impacted by Paul and Silas's decision to fully occupy their prison space. The next morning, after getting word from the community leaders, the jailer tells Paul and Silas, "The magistrates sent word to let you go; therefore come out now and go in peace" (v. 36). Go in peace. When we choose to stay in suffering rather than plot our escape, we experience deliverance and can go in peace.

In October 2016, a month before I entered my suffering space, I accepted an offer to travel with a group to Israel. The trip happened five months later, after my father had passed. Our flight to Israel was amazingly scheduled on the day I turned forty. My brother and husband filled in to care for my kids and my mom. They essentially said, "Go in peace." Not that I had been completely delivered from that suffering space, but the start of my healing had begun.

I cried buckets of tears throughout that trip. But a significant memory for me happened while I was sitting in the Garden of Gethsemane. I understood how we can hold the tension between being sad at loss and hopeful at future glory because Jesus understood that place of the "not yet." In the same garden, Jesus cried tears of blood and asked His father to remove the cup of pain and suffering from Him. And Jesus, being God, knew how the story ended! He knew He would rise again in three days. He knew the second return would happen and He would reign as King of Kings. And yet . . . He grieved the reality of the impending trial.

Even though I know I will see my father when I get to heaven, I can be sad today. I can also accept the suffering in my life and believe there is a bigger plan in play.

The classic graduation verse is "For surely I know the plans I have for you, says the LORD, plans for your welfare and not for harm, to give you a future with hope" (Jer. 29:11). But right before that, Jeremiah tells the Israelites they are going to be in Babylon for a while. Seventy years, in fact. He gives them instructions on how to fill the space while they wait:

> Build houses and live in them; plant gardens and eat what they produce. Take wives and have sons and daughters; take wives for your sons, and give your daughters in marriage, that they may bear sons and daughters; multiply there, and do not decrease. But seek the welfare of the city where I have sent you into exile, and pray to the LORD on its behalf, for in its welfare you will find your welfare. (vv. 5–7)

Basically, settle into the space. Don't just plant gardens, harvest them, and eat from them. Don't just marry off your kids, have grandchildren. My favorite instruction: Pray for the space.

When we go into suffering spaces, we are not alone. But also, because we carry God in us, we can be a blessing, even in those places. On March 5, 2021, a few weeks after my friend Cari's diagnosis of multiple sclerosis, I texted her: "Praying right now during your infusion for God to move through the treatment. To heal the lesions. To do the miraculous." I am not lying that on March 5, 2022, I was standing and worshiping with Cari, crying tears of joy. Just two days earlier at a neurology appointment, she was told that there was no indication of multiple sclerosis in her body.

In Ezekiel 34, God declares enough is enough. He will now be the guide for His people. "I will . . . gather them from the countries and bring them into their own land. . . . I myself will be the shepherd of my sheep, and I will make them lie down. . . . I will seek the lost, and I will bring back the strays, and I will bind up the injured" (vv. 13, 15–16). God is the One who seeks, gathers, and binds up. He sent Jesus to lead the way back to Him.

In my journey through suffering, I've found comfort in looking at Jesus's path, which includes brokenness. Christ's death on the cross was a way out of the pain. Like a good shepherd, Jesus goes first. He never asks us to go anywhere He isn't willing to occupy.

DISCUSSION QUESTIONS

1. How do you view God leading you? As a shepherd or as a sheepherder?

2. What challenging spaces have you been asked to occupy? Do you recognize God's guiding hand and presence even in the valley of the shadow of death?

3. I shared my own story of bitterness, of believing God got it wrong. What do you currently believe God will get wrong or has gotten wrong? Take time to confess that false belief and accept God's forgiveness.

4. Have you considered how your view of God's character impacts your ability to endure times of suffering? Or how assigning meaning to the suffering empowers you to push through?

5. What are you hoping to be delivered from right now? How could you occupy that space with praying for the welfare of it?

ELEVEN

Permission Granted

I look behind me and you're there,
　　then up ahead and you're there, too—
　　your reassuring presence, coming and going.
This is too much, too wonderful—
　　I can't take it all in!

Psalm 139:5 *The Message*

Fire the confetti cannon—we've made it to the end!

You've taken the time to consider where God has assigned you. Hopefully you feel more satisfied, content, and peaceful knowing you aren't going to miss out. Your current position is not a mistake. Through the Holy Spirit's guidance, your eyes may be more open to the invitations all around you to join God's work right where you are.

Maybe while working through the book, you've felt a prompting to occupy a new space. The boundary lines are moving. You sense the shift. It could be a pull to step out of your comfort zone. It could be a step backward into God's purpose for you. You've found clarity in your next assignment, but you're lacking confidence. Especially if it goes against the norm.

I can 100 percent relate. God led me to an unknown territory of podcasting. Back in 2013 most people didn't even know how to listen to a podcast, so publishing episodes wasn't as intimidating as you'd think. My challenge was believing that recording a podcast was a worthwhile endeavor.

It started as a hobby in the years of caring for lots of littles. Then, as more women started listening, I saw how God used this pastime of mine as a ministry. After years of managing all the aspects of podcast production myself, the show grew in popularity, and I was stretched in my ability to do all the things well.

It was a conversation with fellow podcaster Jamie Ivey that led me to the next space God had for me. She encouraged me to value my time and skills enough to consider the podcast as a business. In order to continue to successfully run this growing business, I needed to expand my team. Hiring people to work with me meant moving into the for-profit space. It was the next logical move, but I dragged my feet until Jamie gave me permission. Her words pushed back the voices in my head telling me it was wrong to get paid to do something I loved. *Shouldn't ministry be a sacrifice? Is it okay to get paid to talk about God? Will listeners get upset by my adding "commercials" to the parenting content?*

Honestly, none of those negative thoughts mattered. Because if I had kept spinning all the plates myself to keep the ministry going, I would have quickly burned out. There would be no podcast at all. Now those hesitations seem even sillier since more podcasts are produced by teams and include ads. But when I was standing on the edge of the next space, I needed external permission to move forward. I don't think I'm the only one who needs that nudge.

I have a friend who holds a position of authority in the church and finds herself in rooms filled with men. She's navigating an unfamiliar space, searching for the courage to use her voice where she's been assigned. I have another friend who felt directed to transition from full-time to part-time work. She wonders if she's allowed to not maximize her earning potential, especially if she doesn't have kids. Working part-time gives her time to focus on creative work and volunteer opportunities. Is that okay?

Then there is my friend who has been an empty nester for a decade and feels the desire to get her seminary degree. How will a graduate program welcome a fifty-five-year-old woman? Or a mom of three who feels assigned to homeschool while running her private physical therapy practice. She feels out of place in the homeschool and working worlds but right at home where God has positioned her.

Living life in tune with the Spirit will lead us to seemingly upside-down spaces, like Alice navigating the absurd Wonderland, growing and shrinking and trying to make sense of her experience. We want to follow a formula and believe the next logical step will lead us to a place of contentment. For each of those friends mentioned above, I have generously verbalized my approval and encouragement. While they may nod their heads and absorb my words, their souls long for a bit more. But what if true permission isn't given by those around us or in "how it's always been done"? What if satisfactory permission comes from our position in Christ?

Live, Move, and Have Your Being

The apostle Paul shared his transforming testimony wherever God directed him. One of his most memorable oratory moments happens in the intellectual capital of Athens. After preaching in the synagogue and marketplace, Paul is brought to the Areopagus, which is like their supreme court. (Fun fact: Socrates was condemned and arraigned there.) But Paul isn't on trial. A mix of Epicurean (atheist) and Stoic (pantheist) philosophers ask for an explanation of his teaching. Well, first they call him a "pretentious babbler" (Acts 17:18), the Greek meaning of which gives the image of a bird pecking seeds. They are basically implying that Paul isn't a true philosopher but just piecing together ideas, trying to pass them off as profound.

Despite two directly opposed groups coming together against him, Paul embodies confidence in his assignment. Based on his past experiences (surviving shipwrecks, stoning, and imprisonment), Paul models for us the type of assurance we can carry into our various platforms.

Having toured the city, Paul notes how its residents are dripping in idol worship. Consumed with seeking favor of the gods, they even cover their bases with an altar labeled "To an unknown god" (v. 23). After acknowledging their religious dedication, Paul makes the "unknown" God known to them.

> The God who made the world and everything in it, he who is Lord of heaven and earth, does not live in shrines made by human hands, nor is he served by human hands, as though he needed anything, since he himself gives to all mortals life and breath and all things. (vv. 24–25)

Not only does this statement contradict the Epicureans, who believed matter was eternal and had no creation, it also contradicted the Stoics, who believed God was part of everything and therefore couldn't have created Himself. Paul also rightsizes the Athenians with the truth of who God is: He is served by none. He cannot be contained. He gave life to the philosophers who were trying to make sense of the world He made.

Beyond their excessive idol worship, the Athenians viewed themselves as superior to other communities. So Paul reminds them of their God-given place. "From one ancestor he made all peoples to inhabit the whole earth, and he allotted the times of their existence and the boundaries of the places where they would live" (v. 26). No person is better than another because we all came from one ancestor. No place is better than another because this God sovereignly ordained people on His timeline in their specific spaces.

Paul tells them why God would do this: "so that they would search for God and perhaps fumble about for him and find him—though indeed he is not far from each one of us" (v. 27). In looking for our purpose, we will search for and find God. This God can be known personally.

Then Paul quotes a sixth century BC philosopher-poet: "For 'In him we live and move and have our being'" (v. 28). Not only is God omnipresent (everywhere) and imminent (near to creation), but our belief in Jesus's death and resurrection gives us positional security—in Christ. While the pagan poet is referring to another god, Paul is claiming this phrase for our God.

I want to remind you of the same truth. When you feel insecure in occupying your next assignment, remember, in Christ you live and move and have your being. He gives you eternal life (soul security). He directs your path (a God-listening heart). He knit you together uniquely, for this present moment, empowered by His Spirit (your God-given space).

Your Permission Comes from Your Position in Christ

Just like I said before, Jesus doesn't ask us to do anything He wasn't willing to do first. He left heaven to occupy the God-given space of a baby's body. I can't think of a more vulnerable position to be in: fully dependent on the humans He created to care for Him. But He was willing to experience the discomforts, challenges, and temptations of this earth for you.

Before launching His earthly ministry, Jesus was led into the wilderness by the Holy Spirit. There, the enemy actively questioned Jesus's identity, similar to the way we are taunted and questioned by words that fill our minds before we move into an assignment. Twice, the devil tempted Jesus by starting, "If you are the Son of God . . ." (Matt. 4:3, 6). A third time, the enemy said, "If you will fall down and worship me" (v. 9), again questioning who Jesus was and why He had come. Jesus responded by reminding the devil who God is and of His authority on earth. Jesus's permission came from His position as the Son of God.

Throughout Jesus's life on earth, He often traveled counter to the expected cultural path. He associated with "unclean" people. Others ridiculed Him and His choices, which led Him to the most selfless of spaces to occupy. "And being found in appearance as a human, he humbled himself and became obedient to the point of death—even death on a cross" (Phil. 2:7–8).

Thankfully, the story didn't end with Christ's suffering. Like I tell the children in my Sunday school lessons, Jesus didn't stay dead. His resurrection is the ultimate hope bringer for any space you are hesitant to fill. Because the same power that conquered death lives in you.

More than thirty-five years after the original *Top Gun* movie was released, the newest version, *Top Gun: Maverick*, hit theaters. Spoiler alert: In the first film, Tom Cruise's character, a hotshot pilot named Maverick, loses his best friend, Goose, in a tragic accident while they are ejecting from a plane. In the new movie, Maverick struggles to allow Goose's son, Rooster, to participate in the Top Gun program and fly in a dangerous mission.

I won't spoil this movie for you, but I will tell you that when the film ended, I pulled out my phone and typed in the notes app, "Don't let the fear of repeating past pain keep you from experiencing the redemption story." Like Maverick, we could miss out on the greater good headed our way if we let past pain keep us locked down and paralyzed with fear. God's redemption never ends in death.

Earlier I shared that before my dad passed away, I accepted an invitation for a free trip to the Holy Land. And that at family camp, God brought healing to my grieving heart, turning my mourning into dancing. In addition to those redemption miracles and, perhaps most surprisingly, in exchange for losing my dad, God gave me four replacement dads (and two bonus, female counselor friends). Let me explain.

In September 2020, I received an invitation to join a life team. This group meets once a month for several hours to process life and to learn and support one another. It includes men and women with a variety of professional and church leadership experiences. All but one member are empty nesters.

Humbled by the invitation, my first response was to figure out the logistics of picking up kids from school if I joined the group. It seems silly now. If my worrying about details had caused me to say no to the invitation, I would have missed out on all the love, relationship, and care I've received from this group. These four sixty-year-old men have spoken the words of encouragement I miss hearing from my dad. They championed my first book release. They not only bought copies for all their daughters and daughters-in-law but also read the mom book themselves. They told me how talented I am and how blessed they are by my words.

The two women in the group are licensed professional counselors. Even though these are not technically counseling sessions, their wise advice and perspectives have anchored me during this season. One of them is the mom of four grown boys and such a blessing to my life.

I want to share one more full-circle story. Remember my preteen, homeschooled self, pining away, singing lyrics from *The Little Mermaid*? When I was in eighth grade, I entered a *Brio* magazine writing contest. I shared the story of a time in fifth grade when I called a boy and asked him to "go with me," but he turned me down. To add to that rejection, my story wasn't selected as a winner.

But they did ask if they could publish the picture I'd sent them of my brother and me. I gave my consent. (Even if that pic of me with my arm around my brother's shoulder wasn't a full representation of our sibling relationship, we were cute.) Boy oh boy, was my heart racing when that March 1992 issue arrived and I saw my fave TV show character, D.J. Tanner (a.k.a. actress Candace Cameron Bure), on the front cover. D.J. and I were in the same magazine. I wasn't missing out!

Wouldn't it be just like God to be in the details and orchestrate Candace Cameron Bure offering to write the foreword for my book on being faithful right where you are with what He's given you? You legit can't make this stuff up! In fact, if we let go of our plans and lean into moment-to-moment dependence, we discover He has plans beyond our wildest imagination.

By leaning into God's presence and accepting His invitations, we never miss out on the redeeming work He's doing right where we are. So, here's your permission slip to do uncomfortable and unfamiliar assignments: You are in Christ and Christ is in you. He is redeeming all things. Permission granted. You are right where you belong.

Acknowledgments

To Bruce: It is beyond humbling to consider all the factors of time and space that aligned to bring you and me together. In full cheese fashion, I 100 percent believe "you complete me." None of what I'm doing would be possible without your efficiency, positivity, and strategic thinking. Thank you for encouraging me to occupy my God-given spaces.

To Quade, Price, Watts, and Knox: As a little girl, I could have never imagined this incredibly full life I live as your mom. I love how uniquely God made each of you and can't wait to see where He leads you. Kitchen dance parties forever!

To Team CC—Terry Ledbetter, Dan Bailey, Dick Blaylock, Robin Wantland, Charissa Lopez, and Nancy Houston: I have no words for the way God surprisingly brought you into my life at a time when I desperately needed your constant support and love. I lost one dad and gained four new ones. I have not only one counselor but two. Thank you for holding my grief, breathing life into my weary, dry bones, and reminding me of truth.

To my small-group peeps—Aaron and Amber Lee, Tommy and Kari Simpson, Chris and Abbey Carter, and Randy and Megan Evans: While this book journey was less emotional than the first, you have remained my steady place of encouragement, love, and belonging.

To Angela Kennedy: Thank you for reminding me how I needed to steward this message and not fear setting firm calendar boundaries. Your hugs are supercharged gifts.

To Clark and Erin Morgan: Thank you, Clark, for your enthusiasm about a second book, including fantastic content ideas and titles—one day fiction and/or *Ghost Chicken* will happen. Erin, your laughter is the air I breathe. I'm amazed at how you persevere and bring joy to so many, even when you have gone through a dumpster-fire year.

To Joel Fankhauser: Thank you for committing to read through the Bible in a year so you could tell me about the boring boundary lines section in Joshua.

To Cari Trotter, Courtney DeFeo, Kay Wyma, Sarah Harmeyer, and Karen Harmon: Each of you has inspired the content of this book. Honored to walk this weird internet world with you.

To my Wednesday morning Bible study—Lisa Henry, Andrea Miller, Candace Lyons, Stacey French, Cat Russell, Heidi Nilson, Carolyn Heinrich, Brooke Jackson, Elizabeth Pounds, DeeDee Kiehn, Shanin Wilburn, and Angie Cooper: Thank you, ladies, for helping me process concepts in this book, even when I stopped coming for months to write it.

To my boss babes—Jae Carpenter, Kathryn Morris, and Lindsey Lancaster: Thank you for always showing up with the love that reminds me I do belong. And for being my go-to guides on all things hip and cool.

To Angela Cirroco and Neil Tomba and all my Northwest Bible Church family and staff: Thank you for always giving me space to use my gifts to serve our church community. I feel valued and appreciated as a woman in ministry, and that is no small thing.

To Candace Cameron Bure: Thank you for being open to God's leading in the spaces He's given you. I'm grateful for how God has used our work together to remind me that I am seen and known by my almighty Creator—a God who orchestrates dazzling details beyond my wildest imagination.

To my DMA Team—Rachael Jamison, Stephanie Snow, Misty Persefield, and Ted Barnett: I LITERALLY could not have written this book without you helping publish the podcast each week. Thank you for bringing all of who you are to encourage women around the world.

To my editor Rachel McRae: Thank you for getting my silly humor. For believing we could do this book thing one more time. And for understanding I could always use a few more days past the deadline.

To the Revell team: Thank you for being open to my wild ideas and kind with your support. Publishing books is no small feat, and y'all helped this mom of four make the book magic happen.

To my agent, Jana Burson: We've been talking about a book on occupying your God-given space for a long time, and she's finally here. Thank you for believing it was something God had assigned for me and for being patient while waiting for me to believe it too.

Notes

Chapter 1 Never Missing Out

1. Jess Connolly and Hayley Morgan, *Wild and Free: A Hope-Filled Anthem for the Woman Who Feels She Is Both Too Much and Never Enough* (Grand Rapids: Zondervan, 2016), 50–51.

2. Henry and Richard Blackaby and Claude V. King, *Experiencing God: Knowing and Doing the Will of God* (Nashville: Lifeway, 1990), 15, 21.

3. Henry and Richard Blackaby, *Seven Realities for Experiencing God* (Nashville: Lifeway, 2014), 17.

4. Kat Armstrong, "Motherhood, Career, & Identity," June 26, 2017, episode 171, *Don't Mom Alone*, audio podcast, https://dontmomalone.com/2017/06/26/motherhood-career-identity-kat-armstrong-ep-171/.

5. Vaneetha Risner, "You Are Not Missing Out," *Vaneetha Risner* (blog), October 26, 2017, https://www.vaneetha.com/journal/you-are-not-missing-out.

Chapter 2 Humbled Success

1. John Powell, *Happiness Is an Inside Job* (Allen, TX: Tabor Publishing, 1989), 6.

2. James Strong, *Strong's Expanded Exhaustive Concordance of the Bible* (Nashville: Thomas Nelson, 2009), s.v. "6041, ani."

3. *Strong's Expanded Exhaustive Concordance*, s.v. "6035, anav."

4. Dave Adamson, *Chasing the Light: 90 Devotions & Photos to Grow Your Faith* (FreelyGive.com, 2016), 16.

5. Rabbi Marc J. Margolius, *"Beha'alotcha Anavah*: Our Precious Place in the Whole Leviticus 8:1-12:16," Mindful Torah for our Time: Meeting Challenges with Clarity and Wisdom, Weekly Torah Study Through Mindfulness and *Middot*, Institute for Jewish Spirituality, 2020, page 2, https://images.shulcloud.com/1239/uploads/Documents/For-Podcast/BehaalotehaHandout2020.pdf.

6. Robert J. Morgan, *The Red Sea Rules: 10 God-Given Strategies for Difficult Times* (Nashville: W Publishing, 2014), 6.

Chapter 3 Boundary Line of Time

1. Edwin A. Abbott, *Flatland: A Romance of Many Dimensions* (originally published in London: Seeley & Co., Ltd., 1884).
2. *Strong's Expanded Exhaustive Concordance*, s.v. "1892, hebel."
3. "Jean-Pierre de Caussade, The Present Moment," in *Devotional Classics: Selected Readings for Individuals and Groups,* ed. Richard J. Foster and James Bryan Smith (San Francisco: Harper Collins, 1989), 201.
4. "Jean-Pierre de Caussade," *Devotional Classics*, 202.
5. Vicki Kraft, "Lessons Learned in 87 Years (Part Two)," June 1, 2015, episode 74, *Don't Mom Alone,* audio podcast, https://dontmomalone.com/2015/06/01/lessons-learned-in-87-years-part-two-vickie-kraft-ep-74/.
6. Don Stewart, answer to "Why Did Jesus Come at That Particular Time in History?," Blue Letter Bible, accessed August 4, 2022, https://www.blueletterbible.org/faq/don_stewart/don_stewart_807.cfm.
7. Kim Cash Tate (@kimcashtate), "This Is for My Older Sisters Who Think You're Too Old to Do What God Is Calling You to Do," Instagram video, February 25, 2022, https://www.instagram.com/reel/Caa-S-1lPfM/?utm_medium=copy_link.
8. J.C. Ryle, "Jesus Came at the Perfect Time?," July 20, 2010, https://www.christianity.com/jesus/birth-of-jesus/roman-world/jesus-came-at-the-perfect-time.html.

Chapter 4 Boundary Line of Place

1. T. Desmond Alexander, *From Eden to the New Jerusalem: An Introduction to Biblical Theology* (Grand Rapids: Kregel, 2008), 79.
2. Barry D. Jones, *Dwell: Life with God for the World* (Downers Grove, IL: InterVarsity Press, 2014), 53.
3. Cornelius Plantinga, *Not the Way It's Supposed to Be: A Breviary of Sin* (Grand Rapids: Eerdmans, 1995), 14.
4. Wikipedia, s.v. "Damocles," last modified August 1, 2022, 12:05, https://en.wikipedia.org/wiki/Damocles.
5. *Strong's Expanded Exhaustive Concordance*, s.v. "4908, mishkan."
6. Rabbi Jonathan Sacks, "On Humility," accessed August 10, 2022, https://www.chabad.org/library/article_cdo/aid/83807/jewish/On-Humility.htm.
7. Steve Bezner (@Bezner), Twitter, January 28, 2022, twitter.com/Bezner/status/14870517859991965?s=20&t=k6DN7xr66YVraEOQjHMgVg.

Chapter 5 Boundary Line of Wiring

1. John Mayer (@JohnMayer), Instagram, September 1, 2021, https://www.instagram.com/p/CTSwYCslK7z/?igshid=YzA2ZDJiZGQ=.
2. Paul's references to spiritual gifts: Romans 12:3–8; 1 Corinthians 12:1–11; Ephesians 4:1–16.
3. Charaia Callabrass (@charaiacallabrass), Instagram, October 12, 2021, https://www.instagram.com/p/CU73Od9LfQS/?utm_source=ig_web_copy_link.
4. Christine Caine (@christinecaine), Instagram, February 22, 2022, https://www.instagram.com/p/CaTSETel2t4/?igshid=YzA2ZDJiZGQ=.

5. *Stand by Me*, directed by Rob Reiner (Culver City, CA: Columbia Pictures, 1986).

6. *Good Will Hunting*, directed by Gus Van Sant (New York: Miramax Films, 1997).

7. Pete Scazzero, "Session 2: Know Yourself That You May Know God," Emotionally Healthy Spirituality Course, 2014, page 6, https://www.emotionallyhealthy .org/wp-content/uploads/2015/10/Session-2-Know-Yourself-Know-God.pdf.

8. "What Are Your Spiritual Gifts," https://www.cru.org/us/en/train-and-grow /quizzes-and-assessments/what-type-of-spiritual-gifts-do-you-have-quiz.html.

Chapter 6 Boundary Line of Experiences

1. *Merriam-Webster*, s.v. "hope (n.)," accessed May 9, 2022, https://www.merriam -webster.com/dictionary/hope.

2. Dr. Curt Thompson, IF:Gathering, Dallas, Texas, March 5, 2022.

3. Dr. Anita Phillips, IF:Gathering, Dallas, Texas, March 5, 2022.

4. Lori Desautels, "How Emotions Affect Learning, Behaviors, and Relationships," Social and Emotional Learning (SEL), Edutopia, March 10, 2016, https://www .edutopia.org/blog/emotions-affect-learning-behavior-relationships-lori-desautels.

5. Jonathan Haidt, *The Happiness Hypothesis* (New York: Basic Books, 2006), 26.

Chapter 7 God-Listening Heart

1. *Strong's Expanded Exhaustive Concordance*, s.v. "3820, leb."

2. *Strong's Expanded Exhaustive Concordance*, s.v. "8087, shema."

3. John Eldredge, *Moving Mountains: Praying with Passion, Confidence and Authority* (Nashville: Thomas Nelson, 2017), 142.

4. Mark and Patti Virkler, *4 Keys to Hearing God's Voice* (Shippensburg, PA: Destiny Image Publishers, 2013), 28.

5. Eldredge, *Moving Mountains*, 141.

6. Virkler, *4 Keys to Hearing God's Voice*, 23.

7. *Strong's Expanded Exhaustive Concordance*, s.v. "6822, tsaphah."

8. *Spider-Man*, directed by Sam Raimi (Culver City, CA: Columbia Pictures, 2002).

9. *Spider-Man: No Way Home*, directed by Jon Watts (Culver City, CA: Sony Pictures, 2021).

10. Amy Rognlie, "Fostering Love: Candace Cartwright Makes a Difference for Bell County Children," *Tex Appeal*, November 26, 2021, https://texappealmag.com /fostering-love-candace-cartwright-makes-a-difference-for-bell-county-children/.

11. Rognlie, "Fostering Love."

Chapter 8 Shrink or Swell

1. Rabbi David Jaffe, "Anava-Humility: Additional Resources for Changing the World from the Inside Out," accessed August 16, 2022, https://rabbidavidjaffe .com/anava-humility/; Alan Morinis, *Everyday Holiness: The Jewish Spiritual Path of Mussar* (Boston: Trumpeter, 2007), chap. 7.

2. Vela Tomba, "Hula Hoop-o-logy (Part 1: Stay in Your Hoop)," June 9, 2014, episode 28, *Don't Mom Alone*, audio podcast, https://dontmomalone.com/2014/06 /09/hula-hoop-o-logy-vela-tomba-gcm-ep-28/.

3. *Strong's Expanded Exhaustive Concordance*, s.v. "1347, ga'own."
4. Hanan Harchol, "The Power of the Earth (Theme: Humility)," video, accessed August 17, 2022, https://www.hananharchol.com/watch-the-power-of-the-earth.
5. Harchol, "The Power of the Earth."
6. Vela Tomba, "Hula Hoop-o-logy (Part 1: Stay in Your Hoop)," blog post, *Don't Mom Alone*, August 5, 2013, https://dontmomalone.com/2013/08/05/hula-hoop-o-logy-part-1-stay-in-your-hoop/.
7. Paul David Tripp, "Habits of a Healthy Marriage," February 11, 2019, episode 234, *Don't Mom Alone*, audio podcast, https://dontmomalone.com/2019/02/11/habits-of-a-healthy-marriage-paul-david-tripp-ep-234/.
8. Tripp, "Habits of a Healthy Marriage."
9. Jeannie Ortega Law, "Filmmaker Shares How Biggest Failure Led to Record-Breaking TV Show about Jesus and His Followers," *Christian Post*, April 17, 2019, https://www.christianpost.com/news/filmmaker-shares-how-biggest-failure-led-to-record-breaking-tv-show-about-jesus-and-his-followers.html.
10. Kate Fowler, "'Sweet' Uber Eats Driver Goes Viral for Going Extra Mile with Kind Gesture," *Newsweek*, January 10, 2022, https://www.newsweek.com/tiktok-uber-eats-driver-texas-donald-jackson-1667360.

Chapter 9 Tending Your Space

1. Shirzad Chamine, "Meet the Judge, Your Master Saboteur," https://www.positiveintelligence.com/saboteurs/.
2. Shirzad Chamine, "The Accomplice Saboteurs," https://www.positiveintelligence.com/saboteurs/.

Chapter 10 Wherever You Go

1. Dr. David and Amanda Erickson (@flourishinghomesandfamilies), Instagram, February 17, 2022, https://www.instagram.com/p/CaFLs-fhg4-/?utm_medium=copy_link, referencing The Lay Artiste, "The Malignant Myth of the Leg-Breaking Shepherd," May 4, 2020, https://thelayartiste.com/2020/05/04/the-malignant-myth-of-the-leg-breaking-shepherd/.
2. Erickson (@flourishinghomesandfamilies), Instagram, February 17, 2022, https://www.instagram.com/p/CaFLs-fhg4-/?utm_medium=copy_link.
3. *Strong's Expanded Exhaustive Concordance*, s.v. "1870, derek."
4. *Strong's Expanded Exhaustive Concordance*, s.v. "8537, tom."
5. *Strong's Expanded Exhaustive Concordance*, s.v. "983, betach."
6. Viktor Frankl, *Man's Search for Meaning* (Boston: Beacon Press, 2006), 66.
7. Frankl, *Man's Search for Meaning*, 82.
8. Frankl, *Man's Search for Meaning*, 22.
9. Timothy Keller (@DailyKeller), Twitter, October 11, 2013, https://twitter.com/DailyKeller/status/388624900111335424?s=20&t=Mg9H_Rrzh2Xffl1dvtx41w.
10. Frankl, *Man's Search for Meaning*, 78.

About
Heather MacFadyen

Heather MacFadyen wrote online before Facebook existed. In 2013, after years of writing blog entries, she launched a trailblazing podcast called *God Centered Mom*. In 2018, the show rebranded to the *Don't Mom Alone* podcast. With over eighteen million downloads, Heather's weekly interviews have been listened to at least once in every country on the planet. In 2021, Heather released her first book, *Don't Mom Alone: Growing the Relationships You Need to Be the Mom You Want to Be*. When she's not recording conversations in her messy closet, she's driving in Dallas traffic, feeding four growing boy-men, or walking around the "hood" with her entrepreneurial husband, Bruce.

CONNECT WITH HEATHER

Find Heather online and listen to her podcast,
Don't Mom Alone, to join a community of moms doing
motherhood together and to get ideas from
sought-after motherhood experts.

HeatherMacFadyen.com

Being a Good Mom Isn't about Doing Everything Right

"*Don't Mom Alone* is a vision to do motherhood with your people! It is a practical guide that will help you find those teammates in the exciting mission of mothering."

—**Jennie Allen**, *New York Times* bestselling author of *Get Out of Your Head* and founder and visionary of IF:Gathering